Architectural Papers III

NATURAL METAPHOR

An Anthology of Essays on
Architecture and Nature

Hiroshi Sugimoto, *Oyster Bay*, 1980.

NATURAL METAPHOR

A la même. [Louise Colet]
Trouville, août 1853. Vendredi soir, 11 heures.

Ce qui me semble à moi le plus haut dans l'art (et le plus difficile) ce ne'est ni de faire rire, ni de faire pleurer, ni de vous mettre en rut ou en fureur, mais d'agir à la facon de la nature, c'est-à-dire de **faire rever**. Aussi les très belles oeuvres ont ce caractère, elles sont sereines d'aspect et incompréhensibles; quant au procédé elles sont immobiles comme des falaises, houleuses comme l'Océan, pleines de frondaisons, de verdures et de murmures comme des bois, tristes comme le désert, bleues comme le ciel. Homère, Rabelais, Michel-Ange, Shakespeare, Goethe m'apparaissent **impitoyables**, cela est sans fond, infini, multiple. Par de petites ouvertures on apercoit des précipices, il y a du noir en bas, du vertige, et cependant quelque chose de singulièrement doux plane sur l'ensemble! c'est l'idéal de la lumière, le sourire du soleil, et c'est calme! [...]

J'aime les oeuvres qui **sentent la sueur**, celles ou l'on voit les muscles à travers le linge et qui marchent pieds nus, ce qui est plus difficile que de porter des bottes, lesquelles bottes sont des moules à usage de podagre, on y cache des ongles tors avec toutes sortes de difformités.

Friday night, 11 o'clock
Trouville, August 26, 1853

What seems to me the highest and the most difficult achievement of art is not to make us laugh or cry, or to rouse our lust or our anger, but to do as nature does – that is, fill us with **wonderment**. The most beautiful works have indeed this quality. They are serene in aspect, incomprehensible. The means by which they act on us are various: they are as unmoving as cliffs, stormy as the ocean, leafy, green, and murmuring as forests, sad as the desert, blue as the sky. Homer, Rabelais, Michelangelo, Shakespeare, and Goethe seem to be **pitiless**. They are bottomless, infinite, multiple. Through small openings we glimpse abysses whose dark depths make us giddy. And yet over the whole there hovers an extraordinary gentleness. It is like the brilliance of light, the smile of the sun, and it is calm.

I like the works of art that **smell of swear**, those that show the muscles under the cloth and go barefoot – which is much more difficult to do than wearing boots, whose molds are just good for fragile feet – you can hide distorted nails and all kinds of deformities.

Gustave Flaubert, *Correspondance: Deuxième Série, 1850-4* (Paris: Louis Conard, 1910) pp 348-9.

Art and architecture have in the course of their long histories repeatedly had recourse to nature as a paradigm for their activity.

Even if art and architecture are, and have always been, exercises of abstraction and cultural artificiality - a dream, a wish, is in many moments present: the aspiration of addressing a potential project that is **"natural" beyond artifice**.[1]

Architecture, in its origins, is a destructive force. Trees are cut down, mountains are transformed into flat lands, the earth is penetrated through the digging of holes for the foundations, ...[2] The destruction-construction dialectical pair thereby acquires a new value parameter, an aspiration today: the desire to create a novel and protective nature, at once comprehensible and beautiful.

Our times have brought further information to these arguments: the increasing awareness of the fragility of our environment, alongside our capacity for physical transformation, make us responsible to imagine projects that establish positive lines of encounter with nature.

At the risk of lapsing into caricature, we could affirm that in the 1960s the "**social phenomenon**" was the recurrent argument, and in the 1980s "**history**" was the point of arrival of the critique of Modernity, as well as simultaneously the possibility of action and consensus in the hands of European social democracy and late American capitalism – then "**nature**" now represents the meeting point of the project and its exterior. Conceiving the project in accordance with the logics of nature means to set it in front of the social registers of our times. This implies the attendant possibility of using shared codes of comprehension, evaluation and, therefore, of collective acceptance, which is particularly necessary in social activities such as the practice of architecture that is in this respect quite remote from artistic autonomy and reverie.

Furthermore, while globalization represents an epistemological cross section of our experience, it also constitutes a considerable strengthening of the hypothesis presented here of the centrality of the reference to nature as a substantial project component. Henceforth, it appears **as a general** argument and also as a support for specificity, for **identity**.

From the operative viewpoint that concerns us here, the project is a synthetic process, which relates and gives form or consistency to a multitude of pressures that are real, though largely gaseous. In this context we must use nature as a **methapor**[3] – that is as a correlate, which marks out horizons of connections in activities and products that are, however, different.

Josep Lluís Mateo
Betlem, storm – August 24, 2007

1 In Latin and Anglo-Germanic languages the opposite of natural (from nature) is artificial (*künstlich*), derived from art (*Kunst*). In this sense, art and nature are direct opposites; the two sides of the coin.

2 In many primitive cultures, rituals to start constructions tried to pacify the violated natural forces. For instance, in all the Andean cultures important rituals, dating from the Inca times and still operating today, establish a precise ordinance that is addressed to the "pachammama" (mother earth) reparation.

3 Metaphor: from the Greek *meta*, over, and *pherein*, to carry or bear. Extension of the meaning of a term, carrying it towards the domain of another.

ESSAYS

NATURE AND ARCHITECTURE

by Philip Ursprung

Fig.1: Joseph Paxton, *Crystal Palace*, London, 1851.

At the latest since not only ecological activists and romantic outsiders, but also politicians and film producers are talking about the threatened nature; since even airlines and car producers claim to be contributing to the protection of the climate, has it become clear that the distribution struggle concerning the inter-mediation of the resource named nature is in full flight. Terms such as "sustainability", "balance" and "bio" are on the advance, gas stations are painted green, and garbage is separated in airport malls. "Nature" as a commodity has massively come in demand. The present high esteem nature as a subject registers offers an occasion to study its history. The notion of "nature", as it was established in the 18th and 19th century, has altered radically through the 20th century.[1] The social, political, technological and economic developments, industrially executed wars, as well as the notion that it lies in the hand of mankind to destroy the earth with weapons of mass destruction, have destroyed the idea of nature as something presupposed and inexhaustible. Unto some observers "nature" can only be thought in inverted commas, or, as American artist Robert Smithson expressed towards the end of the 1960s "simply another 18th and 19th century fiction".[2] If nature is understood as a fiction – be this as a wish for continuity and coherence, be it as a projection of something completely different that may exist – then the question regarding the relationship between nature and architecture arises anew. If nature is not a presupposed entity, but a product of human projection, i.e. something actually produced in the course of industrialisation, then it is something else than a backdrop against which architecture takes place or a raw material that becomes articulate through architecture. The fact that nature can be represented, that it can be reflected through an image, a text or a semiotic system – or, more precisely that it is unthinkable without representation – also contains the option that it can be modified and manipulated. Seen from such an angle, architecture and nature determine each other.

The history of the relation between architecture and nature since the 19th century can be represented in two different manners. On the one hand as the history of forms in architecture; framing, imitating or transforming the specific forms of nature and its forces. Seen from this perspective, Joseph Paxton's *Crystal Palace* at the Great Exhibition of 1851 in London plays a central role. As is generally known, the transept of the building had to be designed in a manner as to spare three old elms in Hyde Park. (Fig.1) These remained unviolated within the glass architecture as an evocation of nature, as an image, so to say, of an entity that in fact had actually been eliminated and destroyed by the architecture. This image of a nature at the same time framed and absorbed by architecture established itself in the 19th and 20th century. From Mies van der Rohe's buildings, which frame the passing of natural time in its daily

Fig.2: Eero Saarinen, *TWA Terminal*, New York, 1956–62.

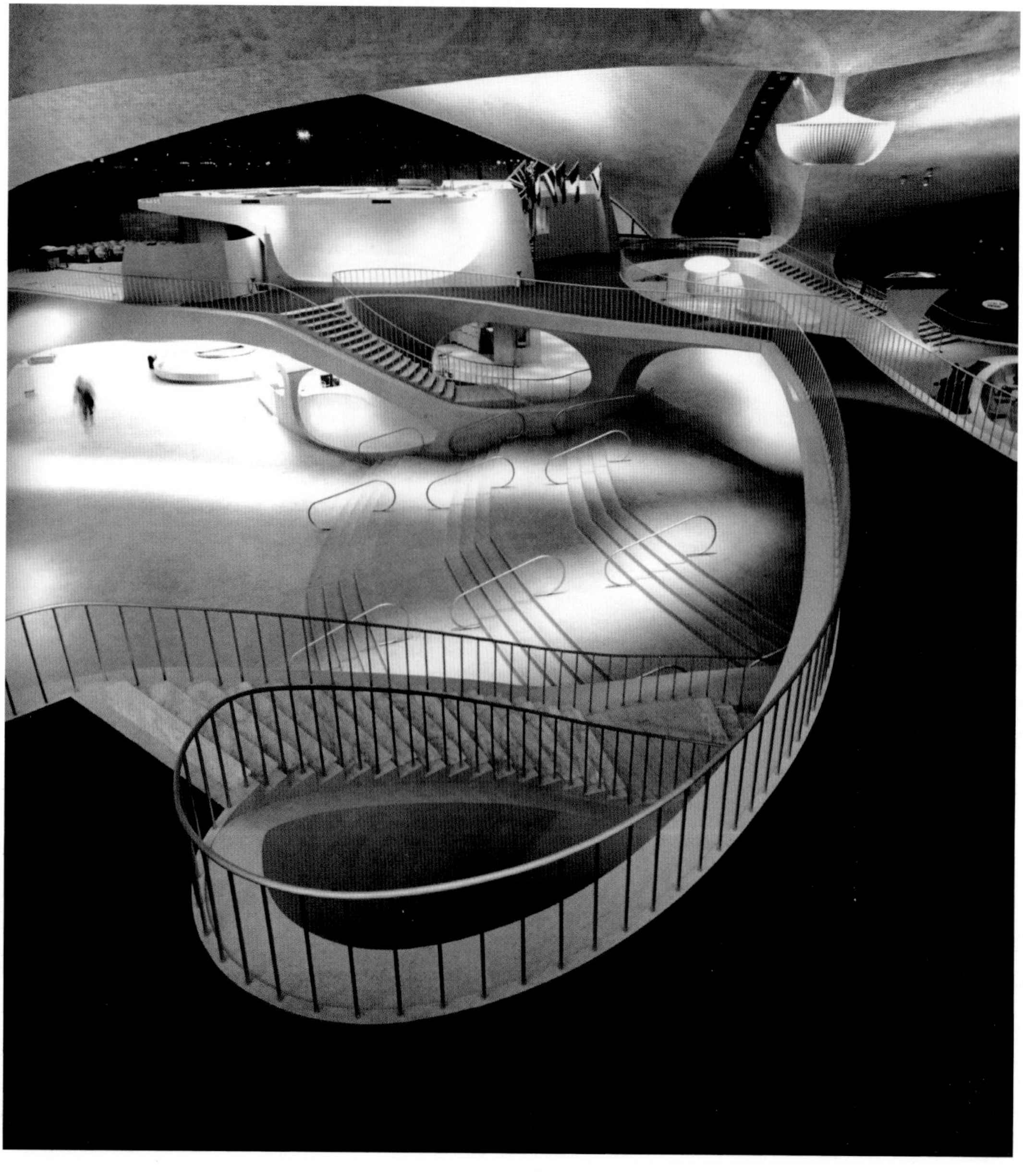

and annual cycle and make them perceivable, all the way to the rubber trees, which are to be found in numerous offices, the tale of dominated nature can be followed through the history of architecture and design. Among the protagonists of the imitation of nature, probably Alvar Aalto and Eero Saarinen have been the most influential in the 20th century. They followed organic shapes in the broadest sense. Their manner of applying the materials – be it wood or be it concrete – reflects the forces of nature, which become visible through the materials, i.e. the force of gravity, tectonics, erosion and growth. Their stance is essentially an anti-modernist position, comparable to those of architects and designers such as Antonio Gaudí, Emile Gallé or Hector Guimard during the end of the 19th century, as they sought reference in those forms that had been suppressed by industrialisation. Their formal vocabulary was universally comprehensible after the mid-twentieth century, and not only popular with specialists, but also with politicians and entrepreneurs. One of the reasons for this was the fact that they found forms suitable for disguising the discontinuity and harshness of Modernism, which lent it a quasi "natural" and familiar appearance. Nature as a metaphor allowed inserting something that in principle is unplaceable into a larger context. Another reason was that their projects always communicated, that the forces of nature essentially could be captured and made accessible to humans, that they were not threatening but available. Saarinen's iconoclastic architecture, such as the TWA Flight Centre in the John F. Kennedy Airport (Fig.2), which reminds of a bird spreading out its wings, his Ingalls Rink in New Haven known as "The Yale Whale" or his Gateway Arch in St. Louis, can immediately be understood by a broad public. Thanks to their evocation of natural models, they create monumental architectures with a capacity for producing identity. Aalto's architectural projects were not least so successful on an international scale, because they have an anthropomorphic quality independent of their size – a vase, a wooden stool, a students home or the plenar hall of the United Nations – and integrate a human reference in even the most abstract political configurations. Besides Aalto and Saarinen, figures such as Arne Jacobsen, Isamu Noguchi, Charles and Ray Eames adhere to this formal tradition, whose effect extends all the way into our present day in the shape of imitative positions such as those represented by Santiago Calatrava or Luigi Colani.

Whilst this is based upon the assumption that nature and architecture are complementary and that architecture may reflect and emulate nature, the other narrative is based upon the proposition that the concepts of nature and architecture are not separate but interlaced inextricably. This notion, which is relevant for the current debate, is based upon the premise that during the 1930s nature became no longer adequately representable as image or shape in the

Fig.3: Schematic Illustration of the *Double Helix*.

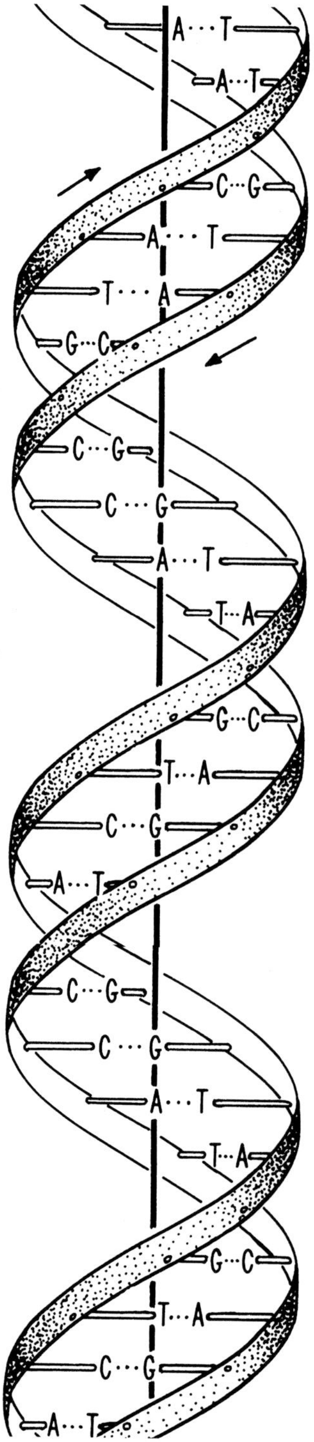

Fig.4: Cover *Life* Magazine, June 10, 1969.

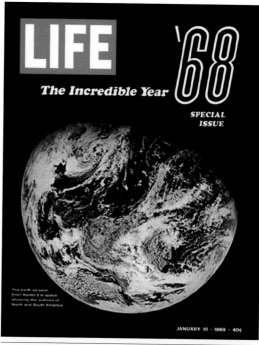

Fig.5: Cover *Whole Earth Catalogue*, Spring 1970.

guise of motives adopted from the realm of plants and animals or as an evocation of the forces of nature. It assumes that the iconographic supply became
exhausted at the end of the 1920s or the beginning of the 1930s, and that nature
had become invisible, as it were. Simultaneously it assumes that figures like
Alto and Saarinen are to be located historically, yet they seem to make less of
an impact seen from a present point of view, as their vocabularies were directed
backward in time.

From such a perspective, nature is just as designed as design is natural;
life is planned in the same way that the plan is something alive. The assumption
that nature and architecture cannot be separated calls for the question regarding their relationship to be argued anew. In such a context, architecture is not
solely to be understood as the theory and practice of a singular building or the
spatial design of our environment, but extends to encompass design, planning
and visualisation of politics, economy, environment, future and human life in
general. The expression describes a series of practices, which directly affect the
control and design of human life, such as genetic engineering, climate control,
birth control, the organisation of associations of nations, the distribution of
risks in insurances and pension schemes, as well as the campaigning strategies
of politicians and the marketing campaigns of fashion corporations.

DOUBLE HELIX AND MOONRISE

A decisive step within this tale regarding the altered view of nature was the
novel representation of the structure of genetic material by the American
biologist James Watson and the British physicist Francis Crick in Cambridge
in 1953. They projected the spatial structure of DNS in the shape of a Double
Helix. Their two metre high model became a new emblem for nature. This was a
spatial representation that not only allowed to understand the mechanisms of
heredity, but also offered the premises for manipulating them – a potential the
researchers actually referred to in *Nature* magazine in 1953: "It has not escaped
our observance that the specific pair structure that we assume immediately
inspires thoughts regarding a possible copying mechanism for genetic material."[3] The effect of the image of the Double Helix upon the public was only to be
registered with a temporal delay, fifteen years after the discovery and five years
after Watson and Crick had received the Nobel prize. In 1968, the publication
of James Watson's bestseller *The Double Helix* made this geometrical figure a
global star. (Fig.3) The message was clear: nature was no longer the mysteri-
ous other, which we are at the mercy of, it had become a language we can learn
to speak and master. We were not to committed to nature anymore, but rather
nature now lay in our hands. By "decoding" the genetic code, as it was referred
to in the language of the cold war in the 1950s, the establishment of a "library
of life" as it was called in the language of the *Empire* around the change of the
millennium, had become feasible.

Fig.6: Richard Buckminster Fuller, *Biosphere*, Montreal, 1967.

The triumph of the Double Helix coincided with another eminent image of nature, i.e. the photographs by NASA of the planet earth. (Fig.4) The proliferation of the pictures taken from Apollo 8, which showed the blue planet in a black universe or a rising earth above a moon horizon influenced the concept of nature for a generation. Nature was visually unfathomably magnified and unfathomably minimised as a system of molecular components on the one hand and as a vulnerable, self-contained system exposed to a vast nothingness on the other side. The term nature was hence replaced by the notion of holistic systems and power relations, of which humans were a part, yet whose continuity and destiny they could partially determine themselves. This shift of scale led to the product becoming less important than the process, the form less important than the function.

Typical events for the shift in design of that period were projects like the *Whole Earth Catalogue,* which appeared between 1969 and the early 1970s; an encyclopaedic collection of objects that should allow to design human environments more favourably, to save limited resources and to develop alternatives to the established forms of industrial life. (Fig.5) The *Whole Earth Catalogue* and the environmental movement forming around that particular time – prominently NGO *Greenpeace*, founded in 1971 – aimed at protecting the fragile system of the earth and established a new lifestyle simultaneously. Paradoxically, corporations pursuing completely different motives succeeded in operating under the sail of this new paradigm. The drastic price increase, which the consumers of the western industrial countries were subjected to, due to measures applied by the international energy corporations and OPEC, the beginning of what is called globalization since the 1990s, was understood by large portions of the public as a "natural" problem, i.e. as an effect of the fact that crude oil resources are finite, and not as a result of ruthless exploitation or the cynical machinations of monopolies.[4] The image of a tiny blue planet was already so intensely established in people's minds that consumers accepted the arbitrary price hike and the consequent economic crisis as a natural phenomenon and did not combat it as a political and economic decision. Genuine global players such as IKEA or Benetton began not only to deliver low-price high-quality furniture and clothes to the international middle classes in the 1970s, but also to establish an international lifestyle, which suggested local identity and incorporated "naturalness".

THE LARGE WHOLE

As the process became more important than the product, the system more important than the form, the event more important than the object, so did the traditional boundaries of trades and professions begin to become blurred. The key figure was Richard Buckminster Fuller, in whose multi-faceted practice the definitions of architecture, art design, theory and fiction became instable.

Fig.7: Friedrich Kiesler, *Endless House*, 1959.

Already in the 1920s had Fuller started to develop new technical visions. His success is inseparably interweaved with the U.S. military industry, for which concepts of mobile architectures were developed, which should function like systems. The emerging concepts for self-sustaining systems – the tensegrity system, for example – were used for military structures such as protective covers for radar antennae, and soon found alternative utilisations in exhibition architecture and mobile forms of housing, which interested the readers of the *Whole Earth Catalogue,* for instance. Buckminster Fuller's utterance "think global, act local" became the slogan of a movement, which at all times remained conscious of its responsibility to the entire system of the earth and was later exploited by the global economy. Fuller's most prominent work, the American pavilion for the 1967 Expo in Montréal, is emblematic for a design that sees itself as an autonomous natural sphere. Until this day, the object named *Biosphère* keeps attracting an audience. (Fig.6)

At first sight, with other words, Fuller's architecture does not adopt any natural shapes. But his concepts all refer to systematic entities, power relations, as well as the relation between humans and their environment. This is comparable to the output of German architect Frei Otto, who became famous through his surface structures in the 1950s. In later publications, Frei Otto explicitly refers to inspiration through natural forms, but his projects, just as his main work the Olympic Stadium in Munich 1972, are like Buckminster Fuller's self-contained systems based upon modular units, in which even the smallest detail corresponds with the whole.

While Fuller and Frei Otto most of all influenced engineers and stood outside the canon of art and architecture history, Friedrich Kiesler was an integrative figure since the 1950s, leaving his marks in the fields of exhibition design, visual art and architecture. His *Endless House* is conceived entirely from the interior spaces and creates spatial boundaries floating into one another; enveloping the inhabitants without submitting them to an arbitrary systematic or aesthetic convention. (Fig.7) For the artists of the late 1950s, Robert Rauschenberg, Allan Kaprow or Claes Oldenburg, for instance, Kiesler was so inspiring, because he articulated *Environments*, which surrounded people with specific material and atmospheric situations, as well as allowed them to modify these surroundings.

Fuller's and Kiesler's activities commenced in the 1930s, even though their effect did not unfold until between the 1950s and the 1970s, and their influence once again became perceptible during the expiring 1990s. If the emerging consciousness regarding the vulnerability of nature sensitised the public for images such as the Double Helix and planet Earth, the question must be discussed, why nature eluded visibility in the 1930s. Why was nature suddenly no longer perceived as form, but as a system? Why are there so many attempts during the phase known as "rappel à l'ordre", to fix an environment perceived as chaotic in clearly defined shapes within the visual culture of the 1930s?

Fig.8: William van Alen, *Chrysler Building*, 1930.

The obsession of artists, architects and designers for monumental forms is
symptomatic for the decay of the old order. This becomes especially clear in
the penchant of the period for crystalline structures. From the surfaces of the
skyscraper facades in New York and the glittering inclusions in the entry hall
of Chrysler Building in New York, all the way to the surface of shellac sheats
and even the musical structure of jazz, a preference for crystalline structures
is to be observed. (Fig.8) It is an emphasis of discontinuity and inner contra-
diction, an alternative image opposing the soft, organic shapes that dominated the visual culture for decades before – and at the same time a reference
to entirely different molecular power processes, which also are to be found in
nature. If the hypothesis is correct that the economic shift of the late 1960s and
early 1970s presents the occasion for establishing a new vision of what nature
is, the destruction of the preceding image of nature could have occurred due
to the economic crisis of 1929. In contrast to the triumph of capitalism and the
beginning of globalization in the early 1970s, whose most eminent image paradoxically is that of the "Oil Crisis", there exists no image for the moment of complete collapse of the economic system, namely the *Great Crash* of 1929. At that
time capitalism experienced a defeat it seeks to avoid by all means ever since.
In its loss of control over the market forces, its nature was exposed for a short
moment – a scandalous, immensely aggressive nature, infinitely more threatening than all thunderstorms, volcanic eruptions and ocean gales together. Never
again, so much was clear unto all, should the market forces remain unbridled.
In the future they had to be controlled and designed. It is this nature, for which
no image may exist in Modernism, which must remain repressed. The history of
the relation between architecture and nature is a function of economic history.

1 This text is based upon my essay "Double Helix and Blue
Planet: The Visualization of Nature in 20th Century" in the
catalogue *Nature Design*, edited by Angeli Sachs, Museum
für Gestaltung Zürich (Baden: Lars Müller, 2007).
2 Robert Smithson, "A Museum of Language in the Vicinity of Art" in: *Art International*, March 1968, reprinted
in: *Robert Smithson – The Collected Writings*, edited by
Jack Flam (Berkeley: University of California Press, 1996)
pp 78–94, here: p 85.
3 J.D. Watson and F.H.C. Crick, "A Structure for Deoxyri-
bose Nucleic Acid", in: *Nature* 171, 25.4.1953, pp 737–738.
4 See the critical account of the energy crisis in *Midnight
Oil: Work, Energy, War, 1972–93*, edited by The Midnight
Notes Collective (San Francisco: Semiotext, 1992).

TREETOPS –
A LEARNING LANDSCAPE

Conversation between Erwin Viray and Jonathan Lin

Film stills from *Early Summer*, Yasujiro Ozu, 1951.

We see the world with our eyes. Our eyes mark the shape of our worlds.

I have been watching Japanese television dramas about high school students. The lectures are never shown. The scenes unfold in between the lives of the students: in the corridors, in the shopping malls, in their homes. As I reflected on these, I recall movies by Yasujiro Ozu. I recall the placement of the camera on an eye level that is the eye level of a Japanese person sitting or more precisely kneeling on a tatami mat. The camera is fixed, the scenes unfold in front of it, actions take place beyond the frame. I recall the experience of entering a two-mat (tatami) Japanese tea room, with a ceiling that almost touched my head. When I was standing it felt cramped and low. But as I sat down on the tatami, the space felt right. My eye-level, as in Ozu's camera, could perceive a different view of the world.

Concurrent with these peregrinations, I imagine the *Asian Landscape*, so vast and so diverse. Perhaps so distinct from Europe, with its idea of unity and diversity explored by Jose Ortega y Gasset.

What is an Asian Landscape seen in the frame of learning architecture? As a teacher, one presumes that pedagogy is based upon the universal idea of equipping the student with the skills necessary for practicing a profession, and to enable the student to develop powers of selection through his/her own powers of judgment. Students as individuals have their own view that may be different from my own. And so I would like to see what they see. I talked to Jonathan Lin, former year one student at the National University of Singapore, Department of Architecture:

How was year one studio?
First year studio consisted of acquiring knowledge and insights into a relatively new subject for freshmen. I would say that during that period one would learn what most architecture students in other schools learn too: basic foundations that run consistent in any school, in any region. Studio sessions involved learning drafting, applying site/contextual analysis and understanding materiality. Studio was also about development, acquisition of knowledge, which naturally led to its application to projects. Design tasks were focused on actual sites in Singapore and were extensive in testing the students' ability to integrate what they learn into their own individual product. To put it simple, everyone receives the same education but generates his individual design through his own context.

The formative period in a studio environment allowed for interaction with tutors and fellow freshmen. Along with the various influences beyond curriculum (architectural websites, journals and personal field trips) one then begins to develop individual working techniques and methodologies.

While working on projects one can test such techniques and assess, refine and hone a "style". Style among the first years does not just refer to an aesthetic, but is more of a slang word refering to an approach to things, to design, to analysis and sometimes even odd sleeping hours (which all architecture students will understand). Our tutors often encourage us to "go out and see the world"; the reason being to gain experience and broaden our views, not just to understand what is happening outside, but also to appreciate and develop a better understanding of our own environment. It allows a student to place himself within the bigger picture of things. When traveling the entire south east of Asia, it would allow me to understand better the multi-cultural environment I live in. Personally I felt that this was essential to becoming an architect in such a melting pot of context.

What is it like to do "Treetops" at the Istana park?
Being presented with a real project that had to be constructed and presented to the public was like throwing us into the deep end of the pool. We were removed from our comfort zones and from the safe environment of studio work. The idea of actual construction and scheduling, meeting up with various clients, contractors and authorities, although scary, was exciting. Filled with enthusiasm, we could finally experiment with new ideas in a real world.

   With free rein and minimal interventions by the tutors (only taking on the role of an advisor rather than a teacher) we had to form our own organization and work schedule, adopting our own approach to the project. Since it was held during the term break, the main aim was to have fun while learning, enjoying the freedom in designing and seeing through a real project. Meetings among us were casual: no hierarchy, everyone had a say in the design, and experimentation was standard. Paradoxically, the real world constraints of such projects provided the chance to develop new ideas that were not taught. A tight budget, paired with minimal construction experience among the team members, forced the students to go beyond common and costly materials. Accordingly, the idea of deriving a form and then developing a construction strategy was also thrown away. Modeling and form-making focused on the construction technique rather than the final form, on the idea of ease of construction and temporary structures.

   Constraints such as minimal digging on site forced students to think beyond conventional foundation concepts. The pavilion would have to be made of light materials that could provide adequate shade from the sun and also create an interactive play area for children exploring the park. With an open stilt structure that in strength gains its seemingly random arrangement of beams and a maze made of recycled wood that occupies a large portion of the site, the building is baseless, and users walk on the grass right into exhibits, which are located under a light cloth canopy. A maze forces visitors to make turns, constantly shifting views, allowing them to experience the vastness of the park from a fresh perspective. From afar, an image of a light and open building is created, where children would be playing in and on the maze, as each maze component is not fixed in the ground, but can be reconfigured to their fancy.

The team realized the need to change the design and sometimes even the conceptual ideas in order to see through the whole project. Compromise? Maybe, but we can certainly call it a rigorous review and correction of our ideas – that not everything we do is always right in the eyes of the client, the public. We no longer just have tutors to review us, which is an added dimension that classroom projects just do not provide.

The final construction and opening of the pavilion to the public was a new experience for the entire team. With only three days of construction, we worked with tight schedules that relied heavily on good teamwork and management. Early mornings and hot afternoons were not favorable. With everyone wanting to see through a project, all worked on for three months. There was a passion to complete what we had started that could probably not have been achieved under any studio conditions.

Jonathan's words give a picture of an Asian Landscape of architectural learning. Reading these words, I reflect on what Josep Lluís Mateo stated regarding the studio at ETH Zurich as a stage set, where the student is given the world in order to face the unexpected, to formulate questions and find answers. The teacher's role then is to direct the students in finding the correct answers. Elia Zenghelis emphasizes the importance of imparting unto students the basic knowledge of the discipline. It is crucial that the students know the facts: the dates, the names, etc., in order to be able to develop their own judgment and make their choices for contemporaneous responses to contemporary needs of life. At the Architectural Association in London, Anthony Vidler stated the importance of history by saying that the most interesting and brilliant practitioners within architecture are also eminent historians.

Under such a pretext, I see no difference in the aim of defining new approaches for architectural learning. Simultaneously I asked, whether there is a difference in the mental landscape that guides the forms and configurations in a particular geography? In the preface to *The Order of Things* Michel Foucault credits Jorge Luis Borges' passage as a passage that shattered all the familiar landmarks of thought, "our thought, the thought that bears the stamp of our age and our geography – breaking up all the ordered surfaces and all the planes with which we are accustomed to tame the wild profusion of existing things, and continuing long afterwards to disturb and

Treetops, Istana Pavilion, Singapore, 2006.

threaten with collapse our age-old distinction between the Same and the
Other". This passage quotes a "certain Chinese encyclopaedia" in which
is written that animals are divided into: (a) belonging to the Emperor, (b)
embalmed, (c) tame, (d) suckling pigs, (e) sirens, (f) fabulous, (g) stray dogs,
(h) included in the present classification, (i) frenzied, (j) innumerable, (k)
drawn with a very fine camelhair brush, (l) etcetera, (m) having just broken
the water pitcher, (n) that from a long way off look like flies. In the strange-
ness of this taxonomy, the thing we apprehend in one great leap, the thing
that, by means of the fable, is demonstrated as the exotic charm of another
system of thought, is the limitation of our own, the stark impossibility of
thinking that."[1] It is a lucid, humorous, and quite disturbing passage on
how the world is seen through our classification of the world, citing Chinese
thoughts in order to set the stage with regard to our pre-conditioned perception of the world. It is most possible that, "Chinese thought is something that
never would construct a world of ideal forms, archetypes, or pure essences
that are separate from reality but incorporate it. The entire reality is seen as
a regulated and continuous process that stems purely from the interaction
of the factors in play." Things can rely on the inherent potential of things
or the situation or configuration of things, that we may call the practice of
the efficacy of things, based on the propensity of things.[2] This is perhaps the
lesson of the Japanese drama, the "Treetops" at Istana Park, and this text
we now are reading.

In *Immemory*, Chris Marker would say: "A more modest, but also more useful enterprise would be to represent each memory with the tools of geography. In each life, there are continents, islands, deserts, dams, overpopulated
countries and unexplored territories. In memory we can represent maps and
landscapes more easily (and more precisely) than songs or stories."[3] This text
is an attempt, a composition with the intent of describing and presenting the
landscape of a certain memory, in a certain place and time, crafting a landscape of learning architecture. In this text an attempt to create an archive is
tested, our world of classification is examined in order to paint one face of an
Asian Landscape that may not be so different from other landscapes of learning architecture.

1 Michel Foucault, *The Order of Things: An Archeology
of Human Sciences* (New York: Vintage Books, 1994) p xv.
2 Francois Jullien, *A Treatise on Efficacy: between Western
and Chinese Thinking* (Honolulu: University of Hawaii
Press, 2004).
3 Nora Alter and Chris Marker, *Contemporary Film Direc-
tors* (Chicago: University of Illinois Press, 2006) p 149.

CHANGE OF NATURE

by Christophe Girot

Idyllic Meadow, Davos.

Why are the words *Landscape Urbanism* and *Topography* so widespread and fashionable in today's society? Could it be that there exists a deep relationship between these words and our irrational yearning for a long lost nature? The reason for such fundamental concerns probably comes from the incredible environmental transformations and upheavals that our world has experienced over the last decades. Never has there been such an outrageous mechanization and systematic degradation of our environment, and never has the question of landscape recovery and repair been so acute, to the point of being irrational at times.

Since its onset, western philosophy has been rooted in the belief of the existence of a primordial state of nature – a nature always capable of revealing its intrinsic and bountiful forces. We have for quite some time been trying to restore such long lost references to idyllic nature in our suburban culture to no avail. The fact of the matter is that the simple natural places, which the archaic Greek so revered, remained sacred and always virginal and untouched. Their belief and philosophy encompassed an effective fusion and a respect for nature. Gathering flowers in a spring meadow was understood as a prayer and nature was simultaneously understood as the place of love and death, of fertility and mystery, of time and its relentless chtonian cycle. In our present society, the massive environmental upheavals have been so overwhelming that such intact and sacred tracts of land are no longer to be found. We therefore need to reinvent the very foundations of our understanding of nature beyond the flowery meadow on the uncertain terrains of the present.

Whether right or wrong, landscape architecture has surfed on the continual disasters of our self-degraded world. It has come to be one of the only design professions capable of dealing with a natural remedy of sorts. What it lacks painfully in terms of design history and theory, it compensates in assertive scientific methodologies. Science has replaced poetry and determinism has simply replaced the mystery of the meadows. From the early picturesque and hygienist model at the onset of the industrial revolution, landscape architecture has evolved into a more abstract and environmentalist model at present. The profession has unfortunately evolved rather uncritically into a global design culture, boastful of its scientific certainties and easy catchwords like "sustainability". But this global landscape design culture remains painfully detached from any palpable cultural specificity with regards to nature. Its approach is far from site specific and can no longer claim to be part of the original "physis" the Greeks referred to. It is a design culture based on a truth system, where simply siding with nature signifies that one is undeniably in the right irrespective of what the result may be.

But even when speaking about a genuine natural restoration, the applied know-how is still painfully incomplete at all levels. The challenge is that it is technically almost impossible to restore a natural meadow to its pristine and virginal condition, when the subsoil has been severely disturbed and altered.

It is as if the flowers themselves knew better, whether or not to reward us with such an idyllic setting. In this particular instance, landscape architecture is all too often misleading by propagating the erroneous image of an ecological nature that is quite removed from our culture. The proposed ecological meadows are more often than not generic and placeless. They cannot render the original poetic resonance of our lost idyllic fields, because what they contain in terms of ecological value, they loose in cultural value and specificity. What is served by the profession today is an alienated form of refurbishment that at best can only be sustainable.

Landscape architecture has contributed indirectly to the significant semantic shift in the word "nature". The profession has evolved from a social and historical approach close to architecture and urban design in the past century, to a more systemic and economically based environmental approach at present. Throughout this period, the word nature was used as the founding block of an environmental doctrine, but remained itself relatively unquestioned. It is generally agreed upon that an original state of nature has indeed been lost, and that we are struggling to restore it somehow. But what if it were precisely the word nature with all its nostalgic connotations, inherited from pre-Socratic times, which were in dire need of questioning and definition today? When the Greeks referred to nature and to its sacred structure, they had living examples of this nature just outside their door. This was the *temenos* of the sacred meadows, springs and caves outside the city, with their ritual calendars and mysteries. This direct reference system to an idyllic nature remained valid well into the English picturesque and pastoral movements of the industrial revolution. Here the coded references to nature were quite effective and clearly traditional. *Central Park* in New York is a sublime example of such a coded nature inlaid within a modern city. But since the late romantic period, there has been a breach, not to mention a rift, between this symbolic understanding of nature and daily reality.

Nature has become drastically impoverished and far less bountiful than before. The reference to an original model is now close to impossible, for it is nowhere to be found. The gradual fragmentation and acceleration of our environment has provoked an integral collapse of our traditional cultural reference to nature. What is the nature that we can find outside our door? The idyllic meadows have disappeared from the fringe of the city. What are we capable of offering instead? Creating a natural reference system from scratch on the dust of our hypercities is no easy task. Numerous artists and landscape architects have attempted to idealize environmental detritus to the rank of nature, but the results lack conviction and mythical resonance.

The challenge is, therefore, to recover a better understanding and respect of what is left of nature, and to make the best of it. The nature that we are now called to create can only be in tune with our present environmental situation. It can no longer be some sort of idealized reference to a nature inherited from the past, call it "dirty realism" if you wish. For it is precisely this obstinate reference to an idealized nature belonging to another era that has enabled us to perpetrate the worst desecration of nature to this day. Nature cannot be elsewhere, it is right here, even if it is aged, mutilated and ailing.

Throughout this paradigm shift in the intrinsic value of nature, landscape architecture has remained rather uncritical about itself and has been overly deterministic in setting its targets. But to address the question of nature, without attempting to reconcile man with his immediate urban environment, seems altogether futile and inconsequent today. This is precisely the point where new words such as "topography" and "landscape urbanism" appear. Topography, which should more appropriately be called topology, has become the direct expression of such a new kind of environment. These new landscape topographies, which have spread across our cities, are very far withdrawn from the pastoral idealism of previous epochs. They are conceived on the uncertain grounds of contemporaneous society, deeply unraveled by mankind, a cultural "terrain vague" of sorts. The topographic approach is in fact the direct expression of a fundamental imbalance between nature and society at present. The grounds are filled-in deep with artifice and the topographies occur precisely where there is nothing natural to be found any more. In this sense topography literally means "drawing new ground". It has nothing to do with the old cartographic meaning that we have grown accustomed to. Landscape topographies sit on top of the "cavetops" of unfathomable urban excavations and concretions. They are at best located on the valueless landfill of vast garbage dumps and contaminated wastelands that we would like to name and sell as nature. Topography is seen here as a tool for environmental rehabilitation. It is also supposed to produce added value in a valueless location. This creation of natural value from nothing is the polar opposite of the idyllic meadow. Here we are duly asked to begin from absolutely nothing and to create something.

The topographic approach to landscape architecture is about remodeling terrain for a new utilization and added value. Floors and facades are made to enable sustainable natural growth and process. Within the city, this translates into the direct cohabitation, not to say juxtaposition, of what can be urban and environmental, in some instances the buildings themselves become green and the ground around them becomes mineral. Modeling the artificial surface crust of the city is at the core of the new approach to landscape topography.

It is highly structural and technical. The topographies in question help prepare almost doomed places for potential future developments. Landscape topography is therefore inherently structural and artificial. At this instance one could say that the artificial terrain follows the program. Why are topographies, micro-topographies and macro-topographies alike so important for the future of landscape architecture? They enable a reduced approach to nature, an approach, which is resolutely detached from any reference to the past.

Recent trends have seen the emergence of a new design approach under the caption of landscape urbanism. Landscape urbanism is not a substitute for landscape architecture, as new urbanism is not a substitute for architecture. However, landscape urbanism is a particular field of urban design that is clearly opposed to that of new urbanism. It is about the fundamental acknowledgement of a *change of nature*. The two approaches towards the urban environment are resolutely antagonistic, both in their understanding of nature and of the city. Landscape urbanism investigates into urban environments through a scientific approach to natural processes and systems on site, whereas new urbanism relies on an idealized historicist discourse as a universal reference system. Both approaches apply design modes that are polar opposites: one relies on the natural forces and constraints at work on a given site to help forge a design process, whereas the other imports classical picturesque references of nature and the romantic city to brand an identity.

Both approaches to urban design deal with similar environmental constraints, such as polluted grounds, deeply excavated terrains, absence of original soil and water. But the solutions proposed are radically different. In the case of landscape urbanism, it is the concern with the immediate environment in its present condition, which is at stake. In this case, the slow regeneration of a degraded place becomes the quintessential aesthetic. The emblematic example of the *Fresh Kills* park project, proposed by Field Operations in New Jersey on the dejected remains of 9/11 in one of the largest rubbish dumps in the world, is a clear case in point. This place will indeed take time to regenerate in order to become a somewhat sustainable natural environment, but it has already reached a highly symbolic value for the city. Landscape urbanism is therefore not only concerned with ecological, but also anthropological correctness in a place where new urbanism would probably have remained mute and at best irrelevant.

If we are to learn anything from our Greek forefathers' approach to nature, it is clearly that each place must have its own story. Therefore, it makes no sense to replicate urban models from elsewhere, when the inherent qualities of a site lay fallow. The great strength of landscape urbanism at present is to attempt to look at each and every site condition at face value and to make the best of it,

thus integrating new architectural projects within the existing forces and natural (or unnatural) conditions of a site. Landscape urbanism is about accepting
the present condition in an impoverished or weakened environment and about
learning how to work with it. It is also about making a new approach towards
nature, which is acceptable to others. Last but not least, it is about returning
a mythical dimension to our contemporary context, albeit considerably altered,
and about acknowledging new forms of nature in our daily lives. The relentless problem with the new urbanism and its attitude towards nature is that it
is retrograde and nostalgic, whilst the imagery used is that of our idyllic pas-
tures. The substrate that lies beneath each project remains buried, hidden and
unresolved. *New urbanism* ought to be called *old urbanism*, because it fundamentally does not accept the truth about a place, but prefers to mask. It is about
trying to replace the odious and the unknown with familiar and easily repeat-
able recipes of an idyllic past. But is it not through the inherent quality of each
site regardless of its condition that we will finally be able to retrieve a deeper
understanding and acceptance of nature today? There is an urgent need to
recognize the deep change of nature that has occurred and to act both consis-
tently against and responsively towards it; only then will it open up towards
new landscapes and a new form of humanity.

Computer-milled working models from the joint venture semester "Landscape and the City" of Christophe Girot and Josep Lluís Mateo (2006).

Model by Michael Bühler and Ramin Mosayebi.

Model by Christoph Heitzmann and David Winzeler.

THE LARGE AREA

by Maria Viñé

Surface as Background for Natural Processes, Günther Vogt, *Park Hyatt Hotel*, Zurich, 2004.

The importance of a conceptual approach towards the open, empty space within urban systems has formed a consensus within the urbanistic debate for quite some time. The development that led to extend the discourse regarding classical models of garden and park premises, as well as squares, started to intensify in the 1960s, when the buzzwords of "large scale", "landscape recycling" and "landscape as a resource" appeared on the scene. The scope of responsibility assigned to landscape architecture suddenly reached out to comprise infrastructure projects, water power plants, quarries and gravel pits. During the 1970s the emphasis started to shift towards ecology: natural reserves and national parks came into the centre of focus. The fascination for natural landscapes also expressed itself in new urban projects, for instance biotopes and ecological plantings were developed in locations that were far too small and unsuitable for such systems. The concept of designed outer spaces seemed to get lost. As a counter-movement to this, public space in an urban context was more vigorously discussed during the late 1980s. This was certainly fuelled by the developments in cities like Barcelona, where mostly architects took on the duty of designing squares, parks and streets in the city within the framework of the Olympic Games of 1992. In the 1990s the increase of consciousness regarding ecology and sustainability, caused by ever more evident environmental damages, led to manifest the necessity for preserving and creating large, free areas within urban territories, as well as of emphasising them as a criteria for the quality of urban life. Large remaining areas, often situated at the fringe of towns or obsolete industrial wastelands, commenced to be integrated into the field of landscape planning. Since then the city seems to have enclosed the presently often uncertain free space. City and landscape do not exclude each other, but are inseparably intertwined. If the future is substantially determined by the formulation and definition of free spaces, one may well ask, how an actual "landscape urbanism" can be realised methodically as a discipline.

We used the winter semester 2007 as an occasion to investigate how and with which methodical instruments a "landscape urbanism" can be developed and how a "landscape architecture" can be implemented in dependence thereof. The question was whether in such a case a reciprocal stance of known urban design methods could be applied, or if it was primarily to think about the free space.

The design of a currently large and unassigned free space along the river Limmat, at the settlement boundary of the periphery of Zurich, formed the backdrop of the debate. The task was to implement a sports and leisure park. The riverbank and the farming areas of the existing development should yield a new spatial ensemble, combined with the new programming of the entire surface. The catalogue of approaches, which is also representative for professional practice, is to be reflected in the following.

The known premise was that the urban space is structured by an infrastructural idea that divides it into smaller spaces, which initiate a process of definition.

Object in the Field, Hideki Yoshimatsu & Archipro Architects, *Cemetery of the Unknown*, Hiroshima, 2002.

This entails the problem that out of the existing context of suburban sprawl an indifferent pattern is further extended. The question remains open, what it should be that is projected into the free space. The traditional notion of creating infrastructure as a base for the further urban development had to be completed with an identity scenario. Though this cannot establish criteria for substantiating the usefulness of an infrastructure, it can at least deliver arguments for what one intends to connect.

The phenomenology of rest and movement as the opposite poles of the situation – the park and the water course on the one hand, leisure areas and sportive activity on the other – formed the potential to conceive the coast line as a new development and influenced the park decisively. The influence of certain specified programme activities in a substantially larger free area presents an opportune occasion for achieving a maximum scope of effect with a minimum amount of investment. The projection of such a position in large scale projects has as a consequence that opposite the clear purpose of a location we find a strategically undetermined location. Hence, determining an exact development can occur on another location without regulation. That, which is known at this stage, is determined in form and location, and opposes a not predefined future as a "crush zone". The determined landscape becomes form, a geometrically defined measure, as if it was a large object in a diffuse open environment. The selective position of working with determination and non-determination in an open space form is a border area in its own right, reducing the opportunity of the design to the necessary. It yields a large space to a local scale, without overwriting it though.

The selective position opposes the implantation of an abstract order. The frequent introduction of a grid or geometrical pattern, parallel bands for instance, will hence gain conciseness in places, which disturb the order due to the existing structures and "deform" them to a specific condition. The capacity of general contents through repetition is contrasted with the formulation of these unique moments. The economy described above is reinstalled surprisingly and in a different context. The defined and typologically discernable landscape becomes an object within the structural grid.

In view of presently available computerised automation, digitisation and moulding technology, the form of a geometrically designed topography, often deducted from a metaphor and set in scene over the entire free space, poses the question regarding scale, material and adequateness of the applied means. What might be applied successfully in fragments, fails in shape of a holistic superstructure. The size of the surface, necessarily a critical mass due to the applied methods, has to be experienced sensually, while it can also be opposed to absurd earth and mass deplacements. The strategy following the digitised post-deconstructivism of the 1990s, which applied forming processes to surfaces, will only free the landscape from a generic formalistic approach to a certain degree. It still restricts the capacity to respond to a specific context and program.

Collage Technic and Spiral Form, Petra Blaisse, *State Detention Center*, Nieuwegein, 1999.

"Rather than searching for nature's laws, landscape architecture interprets nature's appearance and its varying patterns."[1]

From the interpretation of natural phenomena may metaphors be deducted, which may again be translated into abstract patterns or diagrams. A so deduced two-dimensional basic figure functions as the basis for the landscape project. The pattern predefines the limits of the areas. These fall into place to yield an image, which one can only perceive from afar. As soon as one comes closer, one will recognise the actual quality and consistency of the individual, assembled areas.

Through the volatility of nature, taking the time-dimension into account, surfaces can also be understood as a background or an agent for capturing the images of change in the general condition. Depending upon the topography and the consistence of the surface, varying patterns and visual metaphors can come into being due to the interaction with the varying states of nature, such as shadow images or rain water images. Such rather poetic modes of reflection can certainly exert a certain charisma, though they are often connected with two-dimensional perception and the transition into the spatial dimension is not very evident.

The century-old discipline of garden and park design is confronted with a relatively young development of just a few decades, which has fundamentally extended the occupational scope. The increasing complexity and range of tasks to accomplish, settlement and infrastructure planning, as well as ecology in the face of accelerating social development tendencies, simultaneously change the notion of nature and landscape at present. The search for a meaningful application of digital media and adequate representation technologies for landscape spaces are constant companions throughout these developments. With regard to this it is remarkable that one rarely is confronted with three-dimensional visualisations of landscape spaces. Instead of representing newly designed spaces in perspective, one applies reference images of existing projects as a tool to convey ideas. This phenomenon seems to be owed to a predominant conceptual deficit in actual practice, rather than a problem regarding the availability of representation technology. Most of the usual planning paradigms remain bound to two-dimensional concepts.

In current practice the notion and the creation of space as a fundamental of landscape architecture seems to have shifted into the rear. The interaction and superposition of surface materials, topography and vegetation to create three-dimensional spaces, its sequences and limitations, is rarely applied. Spatial concepts, such as visual connections, near and far, tightness and extensiveness, horizon, layering and framing, as they may well be discovered in classical models, i.e. the parks of F. L. Olmsted, often make the impression of being a product of chance today. It seems as if the new challenges and recent developments have blurred the view for the essential. Without transposing the transformation of large areas towards spaces with specific properties back into the centre of the design debate, it will be difficult to conceive projects that achieve the charisma of the classical works of reference.

1 John Dixon Hunt in *Topos*, "On the Perception of the
Term Landscape", No. 47, 2004.

LANDSCAPE AND THE CITY

Project by Mai Komuro

Mai Komuro was a student in the joint venture semester "Landscape and the City" of Christophe Girot and Josep Lluís Mateo (2006). The task was to design a *Sport and Leisure Center* in Schlieren, a village in the suburbs of Zurich.

In opening up the now resticted river course of the Limmat, new spatial qualities arose. Spatial belts – one the river space itself, the other the activity zone in the fields, and the third the void in between – were installed to order and structure the given program. Natural elements, such as trees, plants, grass and gravel, were used to set boundaries and define the different zones. The project's focus shifted towards the visualization of the vast emptiness and its essential nothingness. Its radicalism stems from the disappearence of the architectural object itself, the thoughtful definition of the void, and the sensitive handling of natural materials as architectural elements.

View towards the *Limmat*.

FROZEN MUSIC

by Michal Krzywdziak

Score Sample "Modul 3" – *Ronin*, Nik Bärtsch.

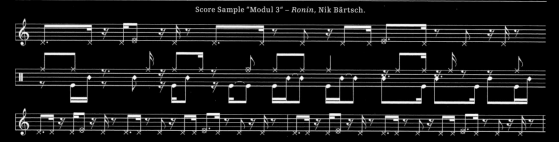

The central phenomenon this piece of writing will circle around is *repetition*, for, as Peter Kivy quotes Heinrich Schenker at the beginning of his essay *The Fine Art of Repetition*: "Our understanding of musical technique would have advanced much further if only someone had asked: where, when and how did music first develop its most striking and distinctive characteristic – repetition?" This technique is closely connected to other terms, specifically module, pattern, structure, reduction and eventually musical minimalism.

There are three musicians I will be referring to in particular. The Russian composer Igor Stravinsky with his *Le Sacre du Printemps* is possibly the inventor of a modular treatment of sonic material. Another crucial figure is the American Steve Reich, who by many is considered the "Godfather" of minimalism. The third musician is the Swiss pianist and composer Nik Bärtsch with his *Ritual Groove Music*, which is also devoted to reduction, repetition, discipline of precision and asceticism.

PETER KIVY'S MULTIDIMENSIONAL "SONIC WALLPAPER"

Peter Kivy states in principal: "The obvious and elementary fact is simply that music alone, from Bach to Brahms, and before and beyond, consists to a large, although of course varying degree, in quite literal repetition of what has been heard before." The author first concentrates on three types of models: the "literary" model, the later "organism" model and the final "wallpaper" model. He tries to prove that the former two do not make much sense as fine arts of repetition, especially in case of what Kivy understands as "absolute music". The characteristic of the "literary" model is its temporal order – a series of events, a narrative nature, and a promise of some semantic value. The "organism" model roots in a metaphor for biological development and the "wallpaper" model perceives its object as "mere decoration or adornment. What perfume is to the nose, or wallpaper is to the eyes, music is to the ears – pleasant, but empty noise".

For at least one reason the "literary" model dilapidates as Kivy claims, "it promises meaning or content, but can never really deliver the goods". The crucial argument against the "organism" model is that from a biological perspective the process of development does not allow a doubling back on itself. This is an operation though, which music permanently uses: "An embryo that repeated the first part of its development all over again would be seen as doing something biologically absurd". The "pitiful wallpaper" model is initially a proposal Immanuel Kant makes in his *Third Critique*, which assigns music, or certainly "all music that is not set to words", to the category of pure and empty decoration without content. Later Eduard Hanslick, untroubled by Kant's apparent trivialization of music as such, would state: "The content of music is tonally moving forms". Following this lead, Peter Kivy draws convincing analogies between compositional repetition in music and the design of patterns on his *Persian Carpet* – analogies, which make sense and are not as tainted with contradictions.

Gilles Deleuze

The first significant conclusion is the temporality of both experiences. The other one is that of a compositional approach – the applied logic of repetition, an order of things, as well as a freedom in perception: "There used to be an unbroken temporal sequence from prescribed beginning to prescribed end, in prescribed order, whereas the prescribed way of looking at my *Persian Carpet* allows a freedom to wander, to linger, to begin where one pleases, and to retrace one's steps as desired." The discoveries finally lead Kivy to define music as a "sonic wallpaper". He names a few features: polyphonic multidimensionality of at least four sonic layers; a quasi-syntactic character of patterns; expressive texture, which means, "the expressive element in music is heard and not only aroused"; and lastly that it is "deeply moving". Eventually, for Kivy repetition as a phenome-non is not "merely an important feature" of music, "but its defining one."

Steve Reich believes in non-narrative structures as well. Talking about *Bikini* he explains: "Instead of telling a story, we'll say that there is a story already there. What you've simply got to do is take pieces of what went on and adjust them. We'll keep coming back over and over them". A similar approach governs the use of text and aphorisms in *You are wherever your thoughts are*: "These texts don't tell a story – but they do certainly make sense together". To use Kivy's metaphor in this instance means that the text samples and aphorisms in both cases become first a motif, then a repeated figure and lastly an combined element on the sonic carpet, where they are, to at least some extent, detached them from their original semantics.

"NON-REPRESENTATIVE DIFFERENCE":
DOES REPETITION MEAN THE BOREDOM OF MONOTONY?

Answers to this question can be traced in the theoretical writings of French philosophers Gilles Deleuze (*Différence et Répétition*) and Henri Lefebvre (*Eléments de Rhytmanalyse: Introduction a la Connaissance des Rythmes*). Lefebvre is convinced that repetition is not at all contradictory to difference, but is even linked to it by resulting from that very technique.

Deleuze probes much deeper. One of the ways he understands repetition is "the continuity afforded by the variation of the intensity in an idea or sensation". He understands "pure difference" as something independent from us, or more precisely, of our actions. Pure difference just occurs. James Williams' explanation is useful in this context: "Deleuze argues that repetition in the arts is not simply the repetition of a motif, as in wallpaper, for example. Instead, each apparent repetition picks up on an element from the previous member of the series and alters it slightly. This dissymmetry is accompanied by sensations that express the underlying movement of intensities and ideas. A virtual dissymmetry always underlines a merely illusory repetition of the same actual thing."

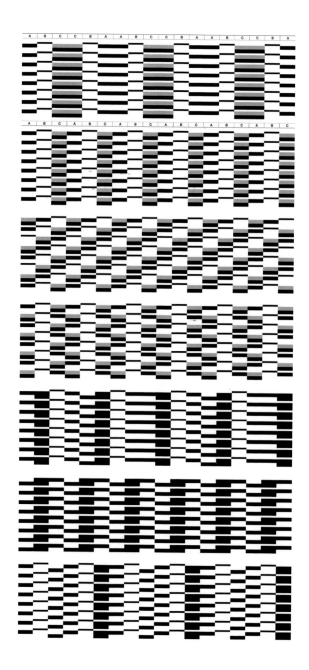

THE ECONOMY OF REPETITION:
THE SEARCH FOR THE POTENTIAL OF THE MINIMAL

The fundamental technique in musical minimalism, apart from repetition, is the use of reductive strategies. Nik Bärtsch shows great interest in that subject. "Reductive strategies are economical, show respect for the material, and coevally free and deepen it. One can listen and look at the material more precisely – how it sings, what it says and how it moves". Bärtsch especially refers to Steve Reich's manner of working in *Piano Phase*. This is an example of the "phasing technique" – a simultaneous interplay of two pianists based on the same score. They start synchronously and continue with one of the musicians speeding up or slowing down. Rhythmically they are consequently coming together and moving apart.

In the field of exploring the potential of the minimal, in a kind of search for the essential, both Bärtsch and Reich admire Stravinsky as the master of efficiency. Apart from being an alternative to the aesthetics of the Baroque form and dealing with the problem of an omnipresent diversity of possibilities, it also entails economical decisions. This was a problem Stravinsky was faced with after the first World War. The recession forced him to deal with minimalism. *Nota bene* Louis Sullivan makes an analogous proposal with his slogan "form follows function", i.e. to focus on and ask questions about the "essence" of problems, which already contain a logic leading to the "form".

THE ENERGY OF REPETITION IN TIME AND THE PROBLEM OF SYMMETRY

A significant characteristic of repetitive techniques in music, apart from an impression of movement or "flow", is the energy it develops in time. Speaking of James Brown, Bärtsch states that "there are pieces by him that go on for 15 minutes, and nothing changes except that they groove more and more. To develop that higher energy takes time". One might claim that repetitive music either arouses a positive response and transforms the listener into a trance-like state of, say, satisfaction, or in a negative sense just "drives him crazy".

Kivy and Deleuze describe this aspect as a dramatic quality or power derived from a progressive movement. Both of them also recognize an enemy of that energy, namely symmetry. Kivy illustrates the problematic in applying the example of the *da capo* aria that registers a symmetrical three-part form of A-B-A. Richard Wagner is probably the most famous critic of that phenomenon: "A repetition of the first part after the middle section is a weakness, which distorts the idea of the work almost past all understanding". On the problem of symmetry and its impact on the dynamics of repetition Deleuze says: "Indeed, it is through symmetry that rectilinear systems limit repetition, preventing infinite progression and maintaining the organic domination of a central point. It is free action, however, which by its essence unleashes the power of repetition as a machinist force that multiplies its effect and pursues an infinite movement".

Hero, Yimou Zhang, 2002.

Referring to his own compositions, Bärtsch points out another interesting aspect, i.e. the spatial impression, which this particular kind of dynamic energy in repetitive music seem to be capable of producing: "The music shows a close affinity to architecturally organized space. A piece of music can be entered and inhabited like a room". Numerous comments on Steve Reich's *Music for 18 Musicians*, a seminal composition in "pattern music" or "sonic minimalism", also emphasize this very feature. Neither is it a coincidence that Reich's composition had an impact on the concept of a genre referred to as "ambient music" (introduced in the late 1970's by Brian Eno with his record *Music for Airports*). "Ambient" in a common sense describes something, which is all around you. As a music-genre, it is characterized by its supposed creation of a "resonant sonic space".

DANCING ABOUT ARCHITECTURE

In relation to architecture it might be asked, whether it is possible to derive new structural principles and strategies for spatial organisation from music. We could reverse Bärtsch's idea of "architecturally organized" sonic space and investigate the potential of a musical understanding of "spatiality". Here for instance the idea of interlocking rhythms or patterns accompanied by progressive movement and transformation seems to conceal possible ways for further investigation. An architect proposing similar spatial intersections, although not referring to music, was Adolf Loos. Introducing the *Raumplan* concept, he three-dimensionally distributed "interlocking" space modules: "I do not design floor plans, facades, sections. I design continuous spaces".

THE END OF REPETITION:
HOW AN "AND" BECOMES AN "END"

One of the key questions concerning the repetition of patterns, based upon the notion of an ongoing flow, is how to end such a composition. Paul Olson emphasizes this aspect of Nik Bärtsch's compositions: "They give the impression that they could go on forever". The possibilities for the listener in Reich's concepts arise from the idea, "that the music is always there and you are just tapping into it for a little while." What you hear is not a framed, finite section of a composition, but rather a revealed fragment of an extended structure. Asked about the tendency of avoiding finality in many of his compositions, Reich states: "There are many ways of ending pieces without getting involved with that. The earlier pieces were basically ended with a "snip" – a sudden stop. *Music for 18 Musicians* does not really cadence, it comes back to where it started. What is really nice about an "end" is when you get a feeling of an "and" – when there is a movement that could be continued. This calls for compositions, which create the impression that it is not the music that stops, but that it is the listener, who decides to stop listening."

MATTER AND TIME

by Toni Gironés

On the following pages I present six exercises, in which **matter** took the design process as the basis for producing a series of geometries. By means of the program these processes then sought to provide a response to given needs.

Paper

"Towards a New Natural Balance"
La Pedrera, Barcelona.

Plastic

Eurofred Warehouse
Cervelló, 1998.

Wood

Eixample District, Barcelona.

Brick

Multi-Family Housing, Badalona.

Stone

La Fornaca Park, Vilassar de Dalt.

People

Passanella, Cadaqués.

The first work involves **paper** – crumpled office paper. In the exhibition/action at *La Pedrera* (Barcelona), a Modernista building designed by Antonio Gaudí, touching the paper and its interaction with light represented an experience for the user. "Towards a new Natural Balance" was based on the four elements of nature: air, water, fire and earth. The crumpled A4 paper as a working unit invaded and filled up the entire space: a fisherman's net on the walls contained it, on the floor a sea of paper laped around our knees, and at the entrance, a printer slowly and deliberately passed out blank sheets. Empty of content, they had a clear message: time is passing. It spoke of order and disorder, to Gaudí's columns, and caressed Jujol's sky of sea.

The main material used in the second project was **plastic**. In late 1998 the company *Eurofred* was looking for ideas for the group's new warehouse in Cervelló. The new warehouse building should increase storage capacity by 16,000 m², promote the corporate image (selling "temperature") and be capable of adapting in time to possible changes of use. The project submitted at the time and completed three years later used the materials to naturally regulate the temperature and define the space by means of light. It was the actual materials that spoke to us of a building, which thanks to its volume, location and simple geometry, interacted as a referent in the collective imaginary: cool in the daytime and warm at night.

The third was **wood**. A narrow street in Barcelona's Eixample district was the site and the program to complement a dwelling: entrance via the garage with swimming pool, changing rooms and terrace. The intention was to take as its departure point the empty space at the centre of the street block, where a garden opens up to the city. A gateway to the terrace was situated at the far end of the plot, using natural light to emphasize the continuity between the street and the garden. Natural cross-ventilation and a degree of transparency conditioned the formalization of the limit with the city. A dry construction used as its main structure corrugated steel that comprised treated timber pressed onto a corrugated mesh. The layout of the terrace on the first floor liberated the maximum space for a variety of purposes. The heated pool and vegetation were situated at the far end, beneath the principal party wall, to achieve maximum depth. The steel and timber fence folded to form a pergola that sheltered the space. A small balcony related to the street, where a pedestrian could walk up to a reedbed along an old stream rather than a building in the city.

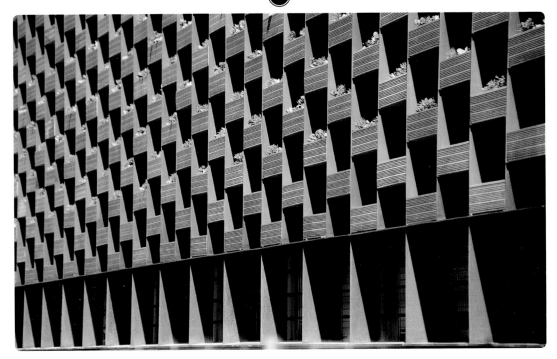

The main material employed in project four is **brick**. An abstract element is a brick lintel
that interacts with the user by modifying and adapting to the different scales of the place.
This project was realized in Badalona, a town with an important industrial tradition that had
grown with the intense wave of migration after the Spanish Civil War. The setting was that of
a town characterized by brick party walls of varying heights that keep up with the processes
of the times. The limits of the intervention were defined by a dry-construction facade, which
recycles a commercial, modular material, namely turning brick lintels. They were transformed
into 1590 planter/window boxes. The project adapted to the layout of the former industrial site,
representing both presence and memory. It retained the envelope as a container, though its use
was very different to the original function (a margarine and chocolate factory), as it now accom-
modated 35 housing units. The window-box element was repeated to adapt to the different functions and generated the final form of the building. The building functions as a biotope that will
gradually be colonized by its inhabitants.

Stone was the material used in this project. The intervention took place in the archaeo-logical excavation site of *La Fornaca Park* in Vilassar de Dalt. The site presented the remains (combustion chambers) of three Roman pottery kilns dating from the 1st century BC. The council had decided to conserve and protect the remains by incorporating a museum program into the new park structure and the existing industrial estate. A feature of our times is the need for programmes at different scales to coexist and interact. It was essential to understand that this "amenity" would attract two types of persons: casual visitors that came to enjoy the park and appreciate the archaeological remains without actually entering, and members of guided tours to visit the interior.

The project set out to respond to all of these variables, leaving the remains underground, where they have stood for many centuries. This was achieved by using a perforated roof, which also formed the main façade as seen from the park. The other face of the "building" presented a section of the site, a geological stratum. The new place should allow visitors to view the remains in their essence – they were almost blind when they entered and had to rely heavily on their other senses of smell, temperature, touch and hearing.

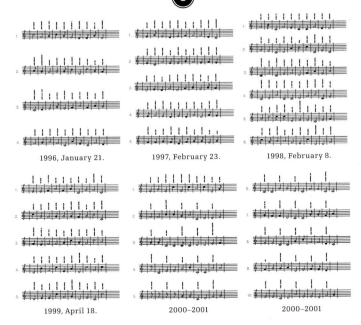

1996, January 21.

1997, February 23.

1998, February 8.

1999, April 18.

2000–2001

2000–2001

The final work speaks of something that I consider fundamental in constituting the mission of each project: **people**, who, as the interpreters of a programme, interact and manifest the countless experiences that inform architecture. "Passanella" is the local name given to the flat slate stones found on the beaches of Cadaqués. It is a normal everyday activity to walk down to the beach, pick up a passanella and try to skim it across the water.

We worked on the sea at a time of the year when it is usually calm: "ses minves des gener", in Catalan, or "the waning tides of January". The intervention comprised a static part, floating elements (buoys) arranged in a 40 x 40-metre grid, and a dynamic part, the ephemeral trails left by the stones as they skimmed across the sea. We superimposed an imaginary pentagram to establish the relation with the acoustic parameters that record the action: the distance thrown determined the pitch, and the number of bounces defined the length of the note. The summation of the various throws produced one of an infinite number of random compositions. Every year the various series' have been recorded, with the name of each person and his musical note.

In general terms this record of the lived place is in any project, be it a building or otherwise, the true function of the architectural space: it intends to be the receptor of time, in which the interaction between matter and energy generates everyday life.

NEW ORLEANS NOW –
DESIGN AND PLANNING
AFTER THE STORM

by *Frederic Schwartz*

Hurricane *Katrina*, 2005.

On August 29th 2005, a monstrous hurricane of biblical proportions fueled
by the climatic warming of the Gulf of Mexico, set its eye on New Orleans,
exposing America's neglect of its aging infrastructure, disappearing coastal
wetlands, deteriorating public housing and its failure to protect its people
– especially its poor. Like New York City's post-9/11 political mess, nature's
wake-up call in New Orleans has been mired in missed opportunities, false
promises, ego, greed, corruption and lack of leadership.

The planning of our cities in the face of disaster (natural and political) must
reach beyond the band-aid of short-term recovery. Disaster offers a unique
opportunity to rethink the planning and politics of our metro-regional areas
– it is a chance to redefine our cities and to reassert values of environmental
care and social justice, of community building and especially of helping the
poor with programs for quality, affordable, sustainable housing.

PUBLIC HOUSING CRISIS

Two years after Hurricane *Katrina*, one of the most pressing and long-term
issues in New Orleans is how to re-direct failed public housing policies (both
federal and local) to best serve the needs of its citizens. The United States
Department of Housing and Urban Development (HUD) and the Housing Authority of New Orleans (HANO) think they have a game plan.

Their idea is to sell prime inner-city tracts of public housing land cleared of all
buildings and give substantial tax incentives to private-sector developers in an
effort to jump start mixed-income projects and bring greatly needed new housing, health and community services to these sites. These are laudable goals, but
while affordable public housing is desperately needed in New Orleans, the faulty
and largely unknown equation of HUD/HANO's 2006 Request for Development
Proposals for these housing areas required a staggering 2/3 reduction in density – 1/3 the number of total housing units then divided into three sectors: 1/3
market-rate, 1/3 affordable and 1/3 assisted. The HUD/HANO equation (1/3 x 1/3)
results in 90% less public housing units! For example, St. Bernard, one of the
largest public housing areas in the New Orleans at 45 units per acre, would be
reduced to just 15 per acre. Under the government's plan, St. Bernard's 1,800 total
units are further reduced to 200 public (assisted) units, 200 affordable units
and 200 market-rate units. The government's reasoning is that current housing
densities breed crime and poverty. False! New York City, for example, America's
densest city also has America's lowest crime rate. As a comparison, we are currently building Harlem's largest new mixed-income housing project (50,000 m^2)
at a density of over 100 units per acre.

Those who question the government's plans also vehemently protest the
destruction of the city's public housing stock that is worthy of revitalization,
because of its architectural, cultural and historic significance and the limited

investment required to upgrade. Two years after Katrina and after much debate, the immediate imperative is to rehabilitate and re-open these still shuttered buildings to afford all former residents of public housing in New Orleans the opportunity to return to their own homes.

UNIFIED NEW ORLEANS PLAN (UNOP)

Following our successful post-9/11 planning in Lower Manhattan and after witnessing the failure of levees and government, our office redirected its energy to New Orleans in an effort to renew this vibrant historic city that suffers from the nation's highest crime rate, unemployment, a failing school system, widespread corruption, racism, as well as the lack of decent rental, public and affordable housing. The citizens of New Orleans recognized our commitment, experience and willingness to help by selecting us in a unique process, where they controlled the final vote in the selection of neighborhood and district planners.

Initial planning efforts in New Orleans repeatedly stalled while people suffered every day through a number of false starts. In August 2006, we were selected as one of four lead planning consultants for the Unified New Orleans Plan (UNOP). Our work included the largest and most diversely populated area in the City (poor to rich, low ground to high, dry to flooded) – Planning District 3 and District 4 (including 21 historic neighborhoods and 43% of New Orleans' post-Katrina population). The work was completed under the auspices of the New Orleans City Planning Commission and funded by the Rockefeller Foundation, the Greater New Orleans Foundation (GNOF) and the Bush/Clinton Fund.

For five months we worked closely with individual residents, neighborhood associations and public agencies, holding over 100 community meetings to plan and submit for citizen approval 50 "bricks and mortar," action-oriented planning proposals for funding by the Louisiana Recovery Authority (LRA) and other state and federal programs. In addition to addressing immediate issues such as infrastructure, housing, open space, sustainability, transportation and safety, we prepared short- and long term planning for both districts and their numerous fine-grain neighborhoods, as well as city-wide initiatives.

INNOVATIVE DESIGN AND PLANNING TO ADDRESS THE HOUSING CRISIS

As the lead planner for District 4, which includes the largest concentration of public housing in the city (Iberville, St. Bernard, Lafitte and B.W. Cooper), we have made every effort to involve the residents and community in the planning effort as a vocal advocate of mixed-income housing that is re-integrated into the neighborhoods through the re-establishment of the historic street grid and strategic architectural and urban interventions.

Our design and planning team started from the premise that every single resident be afforded the opportunity to return to their own neighborhood and that every effort is made to preserve the unique architectural heritage of New Orleans, including public housing buildings of merit. We have been outspoken advocates of affordable, sustainable, quality housing in well-planned mixed-use communities that include retail, community facilities and open space. While density has been a battle cry of those recommending wholesale demolition of the city's public housing areas, density in fact is not the issue – good planning, long-term care, management and maintenance for sustainable community building are.

The return to New Orleans has leveled off at its current population level of 225,000 from 455,000 pre-Katrina and its 1962 high of 627,525, particularly for the lack of housing and vision. As of July 2007, 77,000 potential renters have no homes or units to rent. Of our 50 architectural, urban design and planning initiatives developed for the Unified New Orleans Plan (UNOP), three proposals (one for private homeowners, one for affordable housing and another for public housing) are illustrated to suggest a few innovative ideas to alleviate the city's housing crisis.

3R PUBLIC HOUSING INITIATIVE FOR DISTRICT 4: RENEWAL, RESTORATION AND REDEVELOPMENT

Our public housing initiative for over 4,000 units is an integral part of the District 4 Unified New Orleans Plan (UNOP) that was adopted in May 2007 by the New Orleans City Planning Commission. All four housing project sites, built in the 1940s and 50s, include sensibly planned 2, 3 and 4-storey sturdy red brick buildings with red terra cotta tile roofs shaded by majestic oak trees. The buildings and sites have fallen into disrepair primarily through government neglect and mismanagement, as well as the lack of police, parking, shopping, schools and other community amenities. The pre-Katrina population of these four sites was 99% African-American. This initiative addresses a basic tenet of the Unified New Orleans Plan that promises every resident of New Orleans the right to return home, including all residents of public housing. The goal is to provide a viable mix of affordable, sustainable, quality housing opportunities for renters, workers, public-assisted families and homeowners.

The 3R Affordable and Public Housing Program renews, restores and redevelops all of the major public housing sites in District 4 (Lafitte, B. W. Cooper, St. Bernard, Iberville) by establishing mixed-income neighborhoods. The urban design strategy erases the demarcation of the super block and its association with poverty by re-establishing the street grid and seamlessly re-integrating the surrounding neighborhood by blurring the boundaries between public housing and blocks of historic shotgun and other privately owned or rented homes.

Phased renovation of the majority of significant housing buildings, selective demolition and the strategic addition of new structures, both within the site boundaries and in the surrounding neighborhood, will occur over a three year period.

Existing units will be combined to make larger units, decreasing the total unit density without changing the important total room or population count. New infill housing will be located both within the site and in the adjacent neighborhoods on blighted and vacant properties.

The design of new housing will reflect the look and feel of the surrounding neighborhoods with a mix of both modern interpretations of historic typologies and new urbanist models. It will be built to the highest standards of sustainability and safety, from hurricane winds to flooding. The project will utilize federal public infrastructure funding to offset development costs for the new street grid, sidewalks, landscaping and utilities.

While the Department of Housing and Urban Development (HUD) has declared its intention to rehabilitate and rebuild public housing in New Orleans, our proposal ensures significantly higher density than current HUD HOPE 6 requirements, providing housing to accommodate all displaced former tenants in their own neighborhoods. Higher densities will establish a critical mass to support and retail, public transportation, social services, education and community programs. We call it NEW HOPE.

NEIGHBORHOOD GREEN BLOCK AND HOUSE MOVING PROGRAM

The Neighborhood Green Block and House Moving Program is a city-wide initiative that addresses the lack of neighborhood public open space, the dire need to renew blighted properties and the problems that neighborhoods and homeowners face resulting from the "jack-o-lantern" or "missing teeth" effect caused by scattered run-down, abandoned houses. Using District 4 neighborhoods as an example, this program was developed with and overwhelmingly approved by the citizens and adopted by the New Orleans City Planning Commission as part of our work for the Unified New Orleans Plan (UNOP).

The program operates at a manageable neighborhood scale of 9 blocks (3 by 3 grid) and proposes to physically move all healthy houses (an average of 15 per location) from a 2-acre block in the middle and relocate them to vacant or blighted lots on the surrounding 8 blocks. After relocating the houses, the cleared center block would be redeveloped as a new public open space. Our team is in discussion with The Trust for Public Land's New Orleans office to form a partnership that would program, manage and maintain the new park.

Participants will be compensated 100% with a one-time payment for their building lots and title to the lots where their houses are relocated. House moving costs and interim expenses would also be fully covered. The program would be 100% voluntary, with funds disbursed on a first-come basis from Louisiana's federally funded, multi-billion Dollar road home initiative that provides a one-time tax-deductible payment of up to $150,000 to homeowners that move back and repair their homes or sell their properties outright to the government.

The estimated cost for each neighborhood nine-block area including house moving, administrative and legal fees, landscape and infrastructure is $5 million with the projected start date on the 3rd anniversary of Katrina.

This "triple-win" program creates benefits for individual homeowners, the neighborhoods and the city. Blighted houses and vacant lots are redeveloped to move back into the private market. The public open space network is augmented and improved through the creation of valuable new park land. The program will produce neighborhood-scale planning and design benefits that include filling in undeveloped street corners and "missing teeth," improving property value by forestalling the "jack-o-lantern effect," creating continuous rows of housing and providing safety with "eyes on the street" through increased density and a more mindful neighborhood.

NEW ORLEANS SHOTGUN LOFTHOUSE FOR GLOBAL GREEN

Utilizing existing resources and structures offers a cost-effective, energy-efficient way to help alleviate the housing crisis. Historically, New Orleans's revered "shotgun houses" have weathered the storms and rising waters. By interpreting the effective principles and proportions of these houses, we created a super-sustainable, award-winning new typology for New Orleans.

Our multi-family *Shotgun LoftHouse* reinvents a time-proven climate-driven housing type for both the Holy Cross neighborhood and the city. In terms of its architecture, site planning and economics, the Shotgun LoftHouse is pragmatic, ecological, economical, efficient, innovative, relevant and realistic.

Density and shared party walls minimize the exterior exposure of the units and therefore conserve materials, as well as energy. The building is lifted four feet off the ground for ventilation, positive airflow and flood prevention. The garden-facing elevation is a vertical stacking of deep southern porches with shared stairways covered by lush vines that utilize storm water runoff. Porches facing the Mississippi River are outfitted with a dual-protection shuttering system for the hurricane season. Windows, waterproofing, insulation, air barriers and finishes are prefabricated off-site to insure a tight and efficient building envelope. Roof water collection nourishes a lush landscape that includes filtration pools for treatment of grey water and storm run-off.

The design and construction utilizes regional, renewable and post-Katrina recycled materials (telephone poles, southern pine, recycled steel, recycled wood floors), as well as passive design (cross-unit ventilation and chimney-effect cooling, deep porch shading, green and PV-panel shaded roofs) to reduce energy for cooling (preserves natural resources and reduces carbon emissions). The design, construction and operation factors a 93% reduction in energy costs as compared to standard projects for the multi-family units, while the single family homes will produce more energy than they consume.

Laffite Housing: existing street grid and proposed grid to connect the public housing with the neighborhood.

Historic houses at center moved to surrounding vacant lots; lots filled in and blocks of housing making a whole that faces a new *public park*.

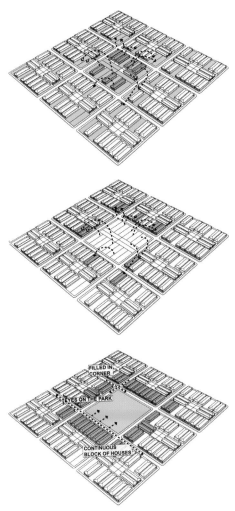

WATER – VALENCIA HEADING FOR THE SEA

by Ramias Steinemann

America's Cup

In the four-element-paradigm introduced by Empedokles and then promoted most of all by Aristotle, *water* is besides fire, air and earth the origin of life. Solid, liquid or gaseous, water is the only chemical compound in the world, which occurs naturally in all three physical states. Due to permanent evaporation, the consequent cooling down of the vapour in the atmosphere and the connected precipitation, water is subject to an ever repeating cycle. The resulting energy from the cycle in the form of wind was utilised by the first seafarers about 7000 years ago. Travelling solely with the power of the wind and buoyancy, they explored the oceans during several thousand years, creating the basis for the present cartographic knowledge of the world.

The great importance of nautical travel for discoveries, commerce, transport and warfare, which prevailed until the 19th century, has yielded to pure sports and leisure sailing in the industrialised countries. In spite of this, water will in future, as in the past, move humans and influence urban architecture.

In Valencia, a city strongly influenced by water, the most important sailing event and the third largest sports event of the world, the *America's Cup*, has taken place in 2007. Valencia's city centre in contrast to other Mediterranean cities did not develop towards the sea, but six kilometres inland from the coast. The city has always had an ambivalent relationship to the ocean. It has developed a similarly difficult relationship with regard to the river *Turia* that was drained after the great flood of 1957 and redirected around the southern edge of the town. Since then the city has been in the dry. The park area between the old town and the estuary mouth baffles tourists and locals alike: besides the "Oceanográfic", a huge water park established by Felix Candela in 1963 that was initially planned as a "science park", there is also the quadripartite ensemble named "Ciutat del les Arts i de les Ciències" built by Santiago Calatrava between 1991 and 2007.

The one that follows the old river bed all the way to the port, passing between the white sceneries, which Calatrava has conceived, stumbling over swards and guard railing, begins to understand, where the future of Valencia lies – namely in the former estuary of the Turia. At the end of this dried-up band between the district *El Cabanyal*, the former estuary of the Turia and the freight port, the first phase of the refurbishment of Valencia has already been finalised. This is the renewal of the port basin with its run-down warehouses. It is this "Darsena" itself and its surroundings, which has now been redesigned as the "Port Americas Cup Marina". In comparison to other European port towns, Valencia is reacting late with regard to this, yet acting all the faster in redefining the purposes of the "Tendez" with its now obsolete inner port premises as an object for commerce and leisure. The goal is to connect the port structure with the sea by creating a direct breakthrough.

This measure creates new public spaces to both sides of the canal – on the beach, as well as in the industrial harbour. Besides a large marina, a large entertainment complex, apartments and a new port for ferries will come into existence.

The Americas Cup with its 13 international sailing teams has acted as a trigger and permanent engine for the newly raised consciousness regarding a connection between the waterfront and the town. After a racing period of three months, the winner of the Challenger Contest will challenge last years winner. In this duel the "king of the seas" will be determined. The winner has the privilege of deciding, where the next such racing event is to take place.

Urban Development

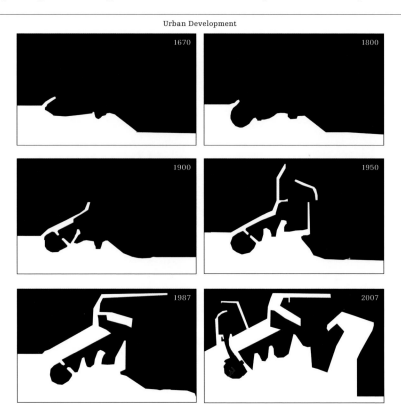

The 20 individual projects by 20 students in their entirety represented the design of the sailing bases with all their necessities. The integral planning of buildings and a complete district was of high importance. Hence, the simultaneous planning of many different sailing bases had a far higher degree of effectiveness in its completeness than the individual object itself.

Comparable to a classical orchestra the voices of several individuals joint in a composition together. Coordination and communication created one large unit consisting of several individual elements. Isolated and for themselves they represented nothing more than functional sailing halls and were without any influence upon the rapidly developing urban texture. The media presence of the event, combined with the large number of sailing bases, lent the measure of realigning towards the new harbour an urban dynamic, without which many other developments in the immediate vicinity would not have been thinkable.

The contrast of the introvert, hermetic halls and the activity outside of the halls, which is directed towards the public, represented the main content of Jaspar Schmidlins work. The conceptual starting point for his project was a "House for a Boat" that especially regards the relation between land and water. Surrounded by competitors, the building was designed as a fence surrounding a courtyard that is open towards the sea. This courtyard was similar to a "pirate bay", where heroes are celebrated after their return. There the team also prepared for its return to the sea. The functional movement of entering and leaving the water with the boat determined the situation and the dimensions of the structure. Towards the land a part of the plot was left to the visitor. This enabled a view onto the port from the narrow street behind the sailing bases and at the same time accentuated a representative entry.

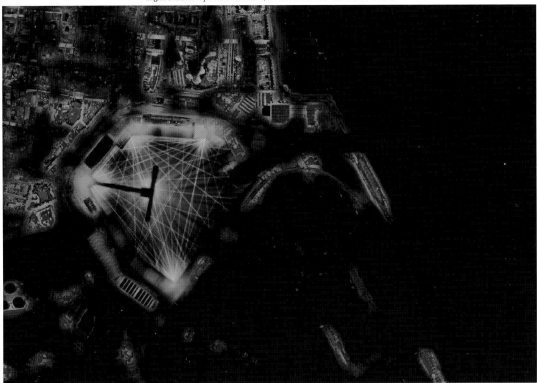

With this exercise it was the intention, through the installation of a superimposed lighting system, to transform the empty vessel of a normal yacht harbour basin into an urban component of the port landscape. The activity on the water and around the basin were made perceivable with the lighting. Light rays were spread to neuralgic points, where visitors gather. They were bundled and distributed radially over the harbour basin in even intervals. The locations, where the rays overlay, appeared as a horizontal light carpet of a sort. As the rays were applied only a few centimetres above the water surface, the moved water surface broke the light and a dynamic structure developed, which played with the density of objects such as boats and the natural elements. Depending upon the strength of the swell, moving the water surface and breaking the horizontal light strips, the sea of light sparkled and flickered in various intensities or rhythms. Without the reflections, which occured on the wave crests, flat light shimmer was to be seen.

EARTH – IN VINO VERITAS

by Alice Hucker

Lavaux – World Heritage Site.

"Terroir" is the expert term for a piece of land, where vines grow. The term signifies a specific combination of material, climatic and topographic factors that apply to a plot of land. It refers to the mineral composition of the soil, the layers of rock below, the height above sea level, the position relative to the sun and the predominant microclimate composed of wind, rain, ground temperature and humidity. The ground has grown over centuries, it is full of myths and qualities, enigmatic and stable. The ground contains a capital, which the vine as a vegetable organism utilises. At the same time it can be experienced sensually by humans. It has a smell, it stores humidity and dispenses it again.

A remarkable phenomenon is the different perception of this constructed landscape depending upon the angle of view. Seen from below the natural rocks of the supportive walls shape a sort of façade. Seen from atop the pattern of the individual plots and the grid of the vine planting dominates the picture. If the viewer is in motion the perception changes anew. Especially then the topographic breaches in the landscape can be experienced with their entire force. The steep slope situation is rival and seducer at the same time. On the one hand the pattern of the vine terraces wash around the interventions, hence substantially isolating them, on the other hand the specific shape of the landscape incorporates new formal ideas.

Every topography forms a relief and is hence ascertainable in its formal qualities. The topographic shape of a vineyard can have a homogeneous progression or develop in a rhythmic movement. It can produce harmonious patterns or chaotic structures. It takes up a dialogue with buildings or other architectural elements that contrast or merge. In interplay with streets and supportive walls it may itself at times already resemble a piece of architecture.

The particularity of the *Lavaux* wine region, which reaches from Lausanne to Vevey-Montreux over a distance of about 15 kilometres is to be noticed immediately. Due to a wine growing culture that is still vital today, terrace-like bands have been created over several centuries running parallel to the coastline of the lake. A symbolic unity of natural and artificial elements has come into being – an artificial topography, which is unique in the world and breathtakingly beautiful. Lavaux is a piece of art, a union of landscape and architecture. The question regarding the dominant and conditioning element is hardly to be answered. It comes as no surprise that the application of this region for an entry in the list of *World Heritage* sites was approved positively by the UNESCO in June 2007. This does not only protect the vine terraces, but also the structures in between. The farming areas here aren't easy to exploit. Their usage is determined primarily by the resulting product, which is the best possible grape quality. One will immediately take notice of the fact that under these special topographic and also infrastructural conditions the Lavaux wines could not exist without the passion of the people.

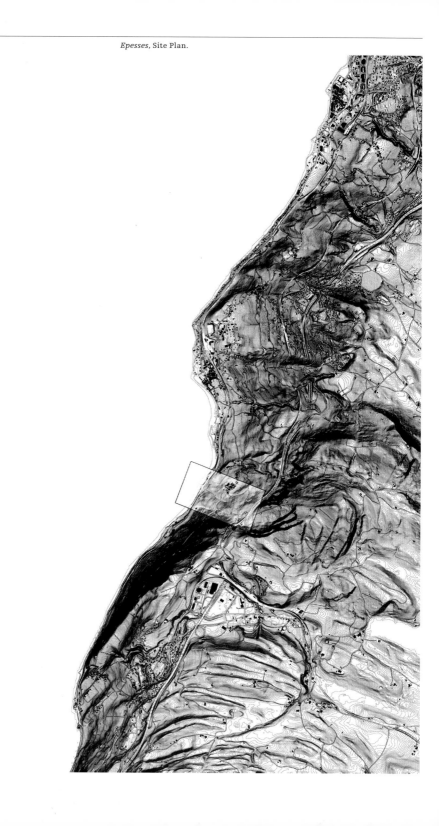

The wine growing culture itself is composed of a natural and an infrastructural work process. Equally important for the quality of the grape are its growth on a good terroir, an optimal production process, as well as a correct storage system. Therefore in order for a good wine to emerge, every vineyard requires a good winery. Like many other sectors, the wine industry is exposed to market conditions, and these are exceedingly dynamic since globalization. In order to prevail in the global price struggle, the production processes of goods are subject to permanent optimisation measures. For the cultivation of wine this most of all entails experimenting with the technical systems, their functionality, size and localisation.

This complex interaction between geographic, cultural and economic factors was the starting point for a study to be carried out during a design course in the studio of Josep Lluís Mateo in 2006. The perimeter of the investigation was set in *Epesses*, a small wine village of the Lavaux region. The task was to establish an architectural design for a winery, which with regard to scale contrasted the existing context. The heterogeneous spatial programme contained all stages of wine production and administration – the premises for wine-tasting, wine-trading and a hotel, as well as an apartment for the winegrowers' family. On the one hand this case study asked for a new image for a winery, on the other side for a new architectural strategy within this concise context. The required size of the new enterprise withdrew the project from the temptation of approaching these sensuous surroundings with too much of a romantic stance.

The design strategies promising the most success can be divided in three groups. While positioning a *monolith* demonstrated great self-confidence within the context, the *continuation of existing structures* with certain innovations attempted to redefine the existing structures. A solution with the largest formal leeway was established by producing a *plateau and ensemble*. Its success lied in the harmony and tension of its individual components. All three presented architectural strategies attempted to utilise the existing qualities of the region. In this case that meant most of all to find an optimal balance between the architecture and the shapes of the landscape. With their large bandwidth, the works of the students tested the possibilities rather than that they offered clear answers. In overall they demonstrate what is at stake for Lavaux, when the local wine industry is exposed to the contemporary forces of the economy. They showed the dangers as well as the chances that lie in all structural interventions.

One can refer to a castle as a historical model for a monolith within a landscape. A profiled volume, which integrates into the few stand-alone structures. The monolith confronts the slope as a levelling moment of sorts. It consumes very little base area and connects with the walls of the vineyard slopes via its materiality (natural rock) in a highly convincing manner.
The transitions from building to landscape are sharp. Therefore the topographic characteristics of the existing context clearly emancipate themselves from the set volume.

The inner structure is optimised with regard to the process of wine production and utilises the force of gravity by its position in the existing slope. In the building the walls let observers experience the relation to the ground – the foundation of the monolith – through the strength of the construction. While the vertical light elements determine orientation in the basement rooms, the tightly set window rhythm emphasises the closeness to the sky in the upper storeys. Storey by storey one is led to a kind of vantage area and seems to float above the landscape.

A very efficient strategy for handling the different scales of the spatial program is to use the production area as a plateau for the outer areas and to position individual structures there. These individual structures form an ensemble that resembles the houses in the villages with regard to scale. Hence they are capable of functioning on their own within the vineyard.

The lower storey integrates itself as one of the many terraces in the landscape pattern. It is only partially built upon and therefore structurally independent. The connections of the diverse programs offer interesting spatial options, without becoming too interdependent though. Continuing the traditional principle of foundation and house, the transitions between the constructed landscape of the wine terraces and the architectural structures merge and become diffuse. The interplay of the building volumes, their transitions with the surroundings, and their proportions constitute the decisive fields of action to create an exciting whole.

An integration into predetermined structures, such as the village, infrastructure buildings or terraces, offers an interesting point of departure. It contains the exact analysis of the existing structures and demands a new interpretation or a further development of the existing, but yet to be classified structure: which parameters are to be assumed and in which form?

Docking onto the town can be successful, if the compactness of the village structure, i.e. its density and sculptural quality is preserved in the process. An adaptation of the exact structure and scale relations is not decisive in the grain, but in the parameters of height, mass and distance. The quality of the unique terrace landscape is not affected by this in any manner. The only occurrence is a displacement of the boundary between village and terroir.

Another work of near archaeological status applies the existing supporting walls as boundary and facade for the building, thereby integrating itself into the earth. Such an approach asks for a high degree of sensitivity. The adjustment of the new functions to the existing structures and vice-versa represents a permanent act of balancing. Closeness to the infrastructure yields much leeway, as a functional connection is basically at hand and the building methods guarantee a common source. The correct adjustment to the topography and the exact joints for docking onto the linear element are the decisive factors with regard to this.

INSULATION CONCRETE

by Patrick Gartmann

Gartmann House, Chur, 2003.

THE IDEA

The effort to leave behind the graphic quality of the multi-layer, monolithic appearance of concrete buildings was again revived in 1998 during the super-vision of a study carried out at the ETH in Zurich. A residential building with a quadratic ground plan, single storey with 50 centimeter thick outer walls and a 50 centimeter thick pyramid roof, was to be made of white coloured *Lecabeton* that had to be greased once a year in order to remain water-resistant. Setting off from this wish projection the idea arose to develop a heat-insulating type of concrete.

The entire case, the roof and the walls should be made of insulation concrete. Everything should consist of the same material – it should carry the load, regulate the climate and insulate. This homogeneous, light and cavernous material mix should be cast in all shapes and enable pervasions, interlacings and convolutions without losing its plastic character. The size and the position of the apertures should decide, whether a body remains perceivable as a whole or if it resolves into its components. Rough shapings or precise sections should vary the plasticity and specify the bodily expression. Plastic architecture should again be rendered possible in spite of heat-insulation directives.

THE POTENTIAL

"The entire case of the house can be produced from one layer – pliable, massive, homogenous and insulating."

This statement conceals an enormous architectonic potential and myriad technical construction options. The wall construction usually applied is a complex, highly developed, multi-layer arrangement, whose structure is decided by specialised planners. Traditional two-shell masonry consists of 12 mono-functional layers, which are delivered by specialists from different profession groups. This prolongs the building period and in concrete buildings the multi-layer structure can cause complex details to arise.

Insulation concrete makes the suit for visible material surfaces and constructions, as well as a plastic appearance evident again. To build with this material means to build with one homogeneous layer. The thickness is determined by artistic, static and physical requirements of the structure. Technical planning is simplified, as the structure to be developed is already available after the shell is retracted.

THE GARTMANN HOUSE

The house is at the foot of Mount Montalin on the periphery of Chur. It is an experiment following the single-layer principle and pursuing new paths with regard to the chosen building materials. All materials are massive and consist of one layer only – hence the entire hull of the structure consists of insulation concrete, all carpentry of massive walnut and all window frames of massive larch wood. Even the heating radiators are made of untreated steel and the lighting consists of round glass bodies or massive cast aluminium.

THE MATERIAL

Insulation concrete is a material consisting of light aggregates that can be manipulated. The aggregate materials influence the density, compression strength, elasticity, heat insulation capacity and most of all the weight of the concrete structure. As light natural additives pumice, tuff and frozen volcanic rock with a high natural porosity, are known. The industrially produced light additives are created through the further processing of natural products (expanded slate, expanded clay) and industrial side products (pelleted flue ash, expanded glass). Concrete with a density below 2000 kg/cubic metre is referred to as "light concrete". Heat-insulating concrete is a high-performance concrete, which distinguishes itself from traditional light concrete through its increased heat-insulating properties that combine with lower strength and lower density. The carrying properties of concrete under exposure to pressure develop in accordance with the strength and rigidity ratio of matrix and additive material. In regular concrete, pressure forces are transferred from grain to grain, in light concrete it is transferred through the matrix. The structure model shows the load transfer in regular concrete with a high rigidity and in light concrete with a lower rigidity. From this it becomes clear that in light concrete the grain is also strained through tensile forces. Breaking of the grain is the most common material failure to be found in light concrete. The pressure resistance of densely structured light concrete is directly determined by the pressure resistance and tensile strength of the additive materials.

After first experiences with insulation concrete containing expanded glass gravel in the construction of the *Meuli House* in Fläsch (architects Valentin Bearth and Andrea Deplazes), we for different reasons searched for a new recipe. On the one hand the expanded glass bound in the cement matrix is endangered by a possible alkali-silicate reaction. This is a chemical reaction between reactive additives (expanded glass) and free alkali in the pore water in the concrete, whose product is an expansive jelly that can destroy the concrete. The effects of the reaction, which takes place over several decades, are not detectable by eye before several years have passed. Additionally the use of mechanically broken expanded glass gravel is not ideal for the loading capacity, as tensile forces can only be absorbed by the additive to a very limited degree. Due to the breaking mechanism is the inner structure of the grain destroyed and microscopic fissures are caused beyond control, which further diminish the tensile strength. These microscopic fissures encourage capillary water accumulation, which again diminishes the heat-insulating properties.

Traditional light concrete that consists of expanded clay and sand does not register such problems. It simply owes too poor insulating properties. Hence the idea was born not only to replace gravel with expanded clay, but also sand with expanded glass in the shape of balls with a diameter of at least two milimeters.

Together with the company *Liapor* the concrete was developed, utilising the climate-regulating properties of expanded clay, which has a good load-bearing capacity and better insulating properties. A cement-bound crystalline clay-glass mixture emerges as a homogeneous, light and cavernous mass. After diverse laboratory and field experiments, where also procedures relevant for building sites were simulated, such as driving with the concrete mixer or vibrating, we had come a step closer to our goal. Due to its low density tend the light additives to swim on top during the mixing process, which leads to a segregation of the materials. This segregation could be averted by using a suitable stabiliser. In all lab and field experiments we changed only one parameter in order to recognise the effect this would have. As all additives are ball-shaped, the concrete can be applied without problems, as it owns very good flowing properties. The chute position should not be more than 50 centimeters when it is brought in. It must be noted that insulating concrete must be vibrated in shorter periods than regular construction concrete. The water/cement ratio of the Liapor/Liaver mixture was astoundingly easy to control, as well as all other relevant material values.

In arming it is useful to apply thin nets or steel rods, as insulating concrete with its bad physical properties is not capable of transmitting the powers of steel rods with large diameters. For the fine fissure distribution as in the Meuli House in Fläsch, fibre arming can be applied, though this will not replace a constructive arming. In the Gartmann House was fibre arming consciously disclaimed in order to obtain clearer knowledge from the arising fissures. Instead of a minimal arming for 45 centimeters thick walls (diameter 14 millimeters, distance 150 millimeters), the arming was substantially reduced (diameter 10 millimeters, distance 150 millimeters). The complete house was produced monolithically, i.e. without dilatation joints. The fissure pattern registered after four years corresponded to the theoretical projections. The fissures from expansions and recessions are continuous and optically recognisable with a width of 0.4 milimeters maximum. An aquiferous fissure, recognizable by light humidity on the inner surface after heavy rain, healed itself through sintering within a year. The covering of the arming is at minimum 4 to 5 centimeters in order to prevent the cavernous insulating concrete from carbonating.

Special attention is to be directed to the after-treatment. The water contained in the light additives and the hydration heat development during the settlement of the concrete cause substantial humidity differences between the core and the fringe zone. Due to this, surface fissures caused through tensile tension can occur. In order to reduce the danger of network-like capillary loss due to high surface evaporation, the walls should remain cased at least four days longer. The ceilings or roofs can be protected against evaporation with a curing and a cover. Due to the thickness of the building elements and the insulation properties of the concrete, the arising hydration-heat is discharged slower than in ordinary concrete. In the core of the newly applied "green" concrete heat accumulation occurs.

In specialised literature is the maximum tolerable temperature indicated with 60°C. The shrinking and creeping of insulating concrete in comparison to regular concrete is more eminent. The values for shrinkage and creeping, which depends on the load, must be increased by approximately 50%. The water saturation, the porosity of the light additives, as well as the cement content influence the degree of shrinkage. The durability of insulation concrete can be compared to that of light concrete. As in the case of light concrete an insufficient condensation, a too high water/cement ratio and segregation of the materials have a negative influence on the durability of insulation concrete. The heat-insulating properties of this concrete enable the production of homogeneously sealed outer walls and roofs consisting of site-mixed concrete in one layer. The air enclosures contained in the light additives yield a heat-insulating effect, which can even be increased by adding air cavern patterns. This means that the more caverns are contained, the lighter the raw density of the mixture will be and the lower hence the heat conductivity. For the shell of the building sealed light mixtures are necessary. This means a tightrope walk between maximum pressure resistance and maximum heat insulation, as pressure resistance behaves proportional to heat conductivity. The limit for a sealed light insulating concrete lies just below a raw density of 1000 kg/cubic metre.

PERSPECTIVE

Further experiments and patterns show that also coloured insulating concrete mixtures can be produced without a loss of properties. Presently the new *National Park Museum* is under construction in Zernez (architect Valerio Olgiati), which is also built with insulation concrete. In order to achieve a bright surface, white cement, bright powdered stone and expanded clay/glass as light additives are used. Cavern-free concrete surfaces cannot be achieved with insulation concrete without using suction sheathing, as the raw density is equal to the raw density of water. Using insulation concrete new possibilities for material-specific architecture are made accessible and layered constructions are complemented by homogeneous ones. In this manner the relationship between the constructive disposition and the architectural expression is extended. From a technical and material-specific point of view a further development of insulation concrete must be welcomed, in order to offer the market a technically more mature product.

Nevertheless insulation concrete will remain a niche product. Not only is this due to the permanently rising requirements regarding insulation, but also because of the high costs compared to ordinary construction concrete. The practically double price is caused by expensive additives, substantially longer sheathing periods and a risk compensation for the contractors. Some development is impossible in pre-fabrication.

It is my vision to take the heaviness out of concrete construction and to handle it in the same manner as one does with prefabricated wood buildings, where the extendable basic structure is errected within a week.

Fig.1: *E-Modul Range* of the matrix and the coarse addition regarding normal and light concrete.
Fig.2: *Structural Model* of the load carrying in normal, light and a concrete with single components of equal rigidity.
Fig.3: *Trajectory Images* of the main tensions of normal and light concrete.
Fig.4: *Insulation Concrete.*

Fig.1

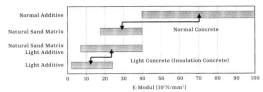

Fig.2

Normal Concrete

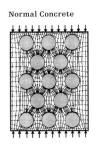

Light Concrete

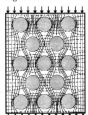

Fig.3

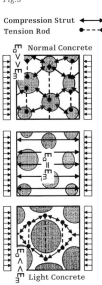

Fig.4

SCENERY OF NATURE

by Catherine Dumont d'Ayot

The following photographs were taken on the occasion of a ETH Zurich seminar week at the chair of Prof. Christian Kerez that focused on the city's architecture of the 1960s.

Jacques Schader, *Kantonschule Freudenberg*, Zurich, 1956–61.

Eduard Neuenschwander, *House and Atelier Neuenschwander*, Gockhausen, 1963–70.

Ernst Gisel, *House Leutert*, Zurich, 1960–1.

Esther and Rudolf Guyer, *Tower at Triemliplatz*, Zurich, 1956–66.

Georges-Pierre Dubois, *Housing Isengrind*, Affoltern, 1967–70.

Jacques Schader, *Kantonschule Freudenberg*, Zurich, 1956–61.

THE SUN ALSO SHINES TODAY

by Florian Sauter

Sand and Stones, 2000.

Nowadays we live in an artificial landscape, where the romantic notion of nature as untouched and idyllic must seem outdated. The classic landscape has been replaced by a dichotomous constellation that uses "nature" as part of a feedback loop with culture. Comparable to an elastic substance, every cultural intervention coevally has natural repercussions. Counteractively they are fused into one and establish a symbiotic entity.

While certain imitations of nature copy its superficial appearance in a formal reproduction, others attempt to decipher its modes of growth. Consequently a fundamental difference between a copy and an imitation prevails: while a copy is only the repetition of a particular object that fails to grasp the idea behind its epiphany, an imitation projects the idea of an object into another object. The latter representation then contains the object's essence in contrast to a plain facsimile. Biomimicry in this respect does not imply copying nature's apparent forms through analogy, but comprehending its structure and methods of production – the obvious consequence then being an absence of verisimilitude or implicit naturalness. Thus, nature can be imitated not in what it makes, but how it makes it – or in other words: one can imitate nature in its action.

Focusing on nature's hidden structures, its rules of growth, two morphological principles of creation might be claimed to exist: on the one hand **optimization**, an internal force that is directed towards achieving the highest degree of efficiency and economy; on the other hand **adaptation**, the organism's ability to adjust to the alternating situations and multiplicity of outer forces. The fusion of these constant, internal laws and the variable, external forces shapes the physical morphogenesis of the material constitution. Entropy in a system is due to the inproportional work in combination, whereupon permanence in a confirmation is explained as a steady "moment" of balance. The current condition might then be understood as the most favorable state in a continuous process of transformation towards structural correctness, authenticity and truthfulness. In its reduction down to the essential, disposal of waste and pursuit of lightness, "beauty" is then the direct expression of the organism's mechanical and geometrical "fitness".

Applying the split strategies of optimization and adaptation to a building, it is comparable to a plant, which simultaneously implements both an efficient and an ambiguous structure. Its material constitution represents a matured organism, where no part can be removed without destroying the whole. Every element of its spatial configuration is interlinked, set into proportion and dependent on one another. Following an organic logic, the building grows out of the ground into its appropriate form. It is rationally developed within its particular situation and cultivated by the holistic forces of the present – the ordinary complexity of reality. Based upon a profound and objective analysis of the specific context and program, the building logically incorporates the energies and resources of the physical world.

Natural architecture accepts difference as an opportunity to modify an ideal, abstract or dogmatic concept into a variety of intricate and ambivalent forms. Compared to the global production of an uniform, homogenous and generic architecture, it enforces the amorphous and heterogeneous through its association with the particular cultural heritage, local identity, social constraints and climatic occurrences. Adhering to no absolute doctrine, its style is to have no style. In a kind of diorama of the profane, familiar and normal, the conceptual focus shifts towards the random, casual and incidental to produce the unique, distinct and special configuration. In its search for clarity in the labyrinthine, its asceticism and anonymity presents an aversion against the exquisite and extravagant. Instead its attitude manifests an original unobtrusiveness and self-evidence beyond rhetoric.

The subjective moment of inspiration and poetic intuition reflects the impossibility of a completely rational architecture. At all times something intangible, not to be fathomed in its transcendental relevance, remains. The instinctive intelligence applied by the vernacular builder must be coupled with the highest forms of technological advancement. Only as a communion of traditional knowledge and contemporary standards, as a synergy that incorporates the high and the low, architecture might offer sustainable answers to apparent questions.

VOICES

CLOSE ENCOUNTER

by Christian Kerez

Florian Sauter has requested Christian Kerez for the photographic contribution on the topic of "Architecture and Nature". From the discussion of the picture selection with Kerez, who had worked as a photographer between 1988 and 1991, this text was created.

At first I show here some photographs from the period before I became an architect. For a long time I did not know what to study. Then, just before my high-school degree, I visited Finland and the landscape impressed me eminently. On an island I took the decision to study architecture. I actually do not know, which was the connection between this landscape and the decision. At least, this landscape had something very architectonic to me. It was not only an extract from an inconceivable whole, but it was constructed in accordance with principles at the same time as it had a wild and enigmatic side to it. Finally it was an irrational decision, which might also reveal the broken reference between architecture and landscape.

The first image shows the house of a whale catcher. It is located on the American West coast, where nobody else builds houses. I always liked it a lot, how the power of the roots lifted the house and how it is nearly destroyed by the tree. The wind is so strong in this area that a threatening closeness to trees promises shelter.

"I find it absurd to use nature as an analogy,
to translate it or to utilize it as a metaphor for architecture.
I believe it is always an expression of weakness,
when an architect uses something else for explaining
his own work than the architecture itself."

The following exposure shows a fortification in Airolo. I find it absurd to use nature as an analogy, to translate it or to utilize it as a metaphor for architecture. These domes here are geometrical structures. Their shape is characterized by the fact that possibly missiles could go down here. Hence, there exists a physical justification for these shapes. The material, everything is made of metre-thick granite, is intended to camouflage the objects. Similar to amoeba, the contours are in relation to the positions of the arms. The entire building is developed logically, using the defence purpose as a starting point. The analogy has no illustrative character. Following a detour via the logics of war, a "scientific object" has been created, which again shows a near random resemblance to this mountain landscape.

At an earlier stage Charles Jencks said that Postmodern architecture is like the frieze of a temple, i.e. the connection of abstraction and pop – imaginative, figurative and symbolic, yet at the same time also abstract and open with regard to metaphors. Now, after some years of aging, the metaphoric has suddenly become natural and is no longer symbolic or historic. I believe it is always an expression of weakness, when an architect uses something else for explaining his own work than the architecture itself. I believe that a metaphor explains nothing and it only replaces an architectonic mystery by an expressive one. In that sense, through the use of a metaphor one enigma is replaced by another one. Whether these metaphors are historic, social or natural is actually of no great importance.

The question is rather, where does this contemporary interest of architecture in nature originate. At the same time I cannot really tell where the interest in history had its roots in the 1970s, or where the interest in art in the 1980s originated. For me references have no meaning – I do not wish to differentiate between form and content. In this sense I am a fundamentalist Modernist.

The next picture shows an English Arts & Crafts house by Edward Schroeder
Prior. He created a lowered garden, sorting out all the stones he found in the subsoil and then mixing concrete with these coarsenesses that eventually covered
the outer facade with a flint stone technique. Now you can of course have the
suspicion that this is decorative and artful in a manner, but the stones he used
were actually collected on location. This immediate reference between architecture and nature is not solely pictorial, no, it is not even recognizable, because
the stones were concealed up to four metres under the ground. This reference
is physical. It is great, because it makes visible the hidden, yet actually existing.

Basically the Modern Age, how I conceive it, bases on two pillars, whereas
both of them are rooted in a total denial of industrialization. One is the Arts
& Crafts, the idealisation of the medieval ages as a god-fearing period without
machines, without over-exploitation and without the destruction of nature.
The other is Japan, with its gardens and its idealisation of the relation between
architecture and nature. Then, the Modern Age in contrast to these two models
accepted industrialisation, so to say as a historical fact, yet retaining the earlier ideology. An ideology that over-estimated and idealised nature. The question where we stand today is difficult, because the exploitation of nature has
led to the present scenarios of catastrophe and apocalypse. I believe that the
first effects of the imminent climatic catastrophe demonstrate clearly that one
cannot do everything with nature and that human activities also have consequences. With regard to this, we are subordinate to nature in two respects:
on one side we cannot really estimate or control the consequences of our actions
with regard to nature, on the other hand we in our lethargy and obtuseness
might also only be comprehensible in our incapability for action – against
better knowledge – as animal beings.

*"It is simply a house and it is difficult to recognise
any architectural ambition behind it. At the core,
the space and the body of the building are the same."*

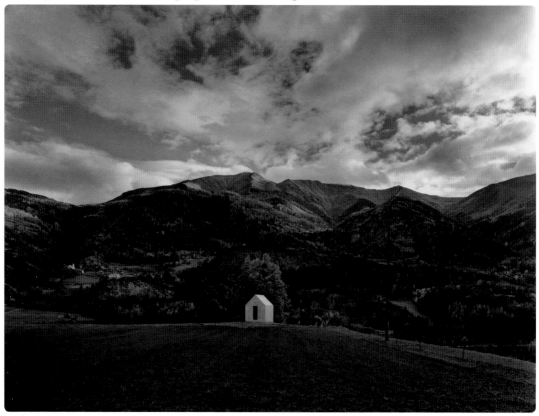

An object, that to me shows an eminent reference between landscape and architecture is the chapel in Oberrealta. In a village or urban context it would be kitschy – "minimal kitsch" – but in this desertion, this overweight of landscape, it actually emphasises the grandness and richness of the landscape through its limited character, its poorness and humbleness. The plasticity of the background has been reinforced readably in the photo. Still it is an accurate photo, as it translates the physical reality.

The chapel is corporeal and every limitation of the volume is clearly visible. If it had for example a flat ending, one would not be able to see the roof. In the case of a cube, as created by Sol Le Witt, one does not know, whether it is a court, a body or a building. The chapel is also in an intellectual sense unobtrusive: it is extremely reduced, like a sculpture, without any details and at the same time conceptually obdurate. It incorporates something helpless or unspectacular in its naivity. It is simply a house and it is difficult to recognise any architectural ambition behind it. Many people reacted by saying that they prefered the landscape on the picture more than the poor project. I actually liked, what some meant a little insultingly.

Inside I attempted to create a directional space. At the same time I did not want to open up the space. It would have been absurd to apply ordinary windows, because just one step further, you have the entire landscape spread out in front of you. Therefore I made a slot so narrow that you cannot look out through it and light can only pass through on its way in. This procedure must also be understood as a kind of protection, as it fades out this landscape for a short period, analogous to a dark break between to pictures.

The slot-shaped aperture is not defined symbolically. It is convex, causing the thickness of the wall to be unperceivable. This makes the aperture mystical too, as everything else in this building is readable directly. At the core, the space and the body of the building are the same. I can just as well understand the inner space as the volume in this project. Later, when occupied with larger projects, this would no longer work. Then, the inner space was the actual project and the rest, the outer appearance, became the derivate of the specifications.

"I am interested in finding necessities.
I seek a compelling, physical relationship to nature."

This photo of the apartment building at the Forsterstrasse was taken by our construction supervisor from a poster by photographer Georg Ärni. It is a landscape within the landscape – the inner space as an outer space is now again located in an outer space.

The Zurichberg landscape is structured by curtains of trees and roads between the plots. The trees always stand where the neighbours do not want to look at each other. The opening of our house must be understood as a reaction towards the closeness of this landscape, this green wall. Every house here dreams of standing alone in the prairie. In order to support this illusion trees are planted. In our case, the idea went as far as to say that these trees and hedges around the house are its outer boundaries.

The environment is incredibly lively and in permanent transformation. Helmut Federle was fascinated that the garden is not accessible for people and wanted to populate it with animals. It is a nice thought that you do not only look out into the garden, but into nature, and that for instance a deer might look back. In the mean time there are many animals that come on their own accord – foxes, many different birds, spotted woodpeckers or squirrels. We are able to distinguish the individual squirrels, as they live here, just as we do.

Nature does not interest me in an ideological or formal manner – not with regard to research and science. My contact with nature is immediate – regardless of whether it is from first, second or third resources. My interest in nature resembles the butcher's interest in cattle. In this sense I also do not have a respect for nature and wish to utilize it in a very basic manner. In the abstraction and harshness of the rooms in this house I recognise a polar correspondence to nature. The grey, colourless nature of the inner space corresponds with the colourful design of the outside. The outside is given a new meaning through the inside and vice-versa. Due to the grey, the colour, the light and the liveliness comes from the outside. This strong contrast is sought for – not in a stylistic sense, but in an existential one.

I always conceive the inner spaces first and the outer shape is rather a consequence of the internal. I am interested in finding necessities. I seek a compelling, physical relationship to nature. For me there is no point in deriving the *Golden Section* from nature or the Fibonacci-row, because at the end there is a rule, which is so general and open that everything becomes legitimate. The force of gravity, which is a natural law, determines large portions of this house. It is a physical conditionality forcing the walls into their relation to each other – it is not a designed one.

"As a physical formation it first appears completely arbitrary. Only the landscape conditions its logic."

One of the most beautiful things I have seen are Scandinavian cemeteries.
A school friend and I travelled around Scandinavia for one month and we visited
a lot of them. The cemeteries appeared very artificial, although they were created
using solely natural materials – some floor slabs and trees organised the whole
area. They neither represent an attempt analogous to English landscape gardening to emulate nature, neither do they seek to intensify nature as does Japanese
gardening, yet they are also not to be perceived as the extension of architecture
with its own means as in French gardens. They are artificially stylised garden
landscapes, created with very anonymous means.

On our journey, we also visited the holiday residence of Gunnar Asplund.
Although it is so small, it relates with the entire landscape – the cliff range in the
background, the view over the fjord and the small court that yields a closed outside space. Also on the inside a cleft in the levels reflects the rocky ground. It is a
house that directly utilises the possibilities of the landscape. We were surprised
by the quality of this house and how wild it appears in reality. As a physical
formation it first appears completely arbitrary. Only the landscape conditions its
logic. This house reflects my interest in nature as a raw material, as well as the
way I wish to utilise it. A work that follows nature as an analogy always not only
reflects a distance from nature, but also a distance from the architecture itself.

THE PRODUCTION OF REALITY

Conversation between Olafur Eliasson and Florian Sauter

Model room, 2003, in cooperation with Einar Thorsteinn, Reykjavik Art Museum – Hafnarhus, 2004.

In the catalogue for your exhibition "The mediated motion" at the Kunsthaus in Bregenz you wrote that the weather is a part of the project. Could you perhaps explain that in more detail?

In my artistic practice I have been focusing on the dematerialization of the object, or the traditional notion of objecthood, which implies an emphasis on the importance of different types of contextual elements. In the Bregenz exhibition, which I did in collaboration with the landscape architect Günther Vogt, there was no distinct border or threshold between the works that I and Günther created for the exhibition, the architecture of the museum, made by Peter Zumthor, the street space outside the building, and even the weather. What I would like to suggest is that an exhibition, whose central part is its experiential properties, includes the whole environment in which it takes place. In this case, the environment was not just the weather, but also the socio-political conditions of Bregenz. The weather was not more important than anything else, but as the show was above all oriented towards natural phenomena, the weather seemed an appropriate dimension to include.

The weather forecast used to be decisive for man's survival. Looking at your work it is striking that this existentialist vision no more seems to be in the foreground, but rather a theatrical staging of climatic events. Would you agree that some of your projects can be interpreted as an artificial representation of the environment?

Well, the skill to foresee the weather was previously related directly to immediate survival. On a cold night one would need to take shelter and during summer one would be able to predict the quality of the crops for harvesting. Throughout history we have developed very different ways of engaging with the climate. In modernity, though, the distinct language involved in predicting the weather and the very direct relationship with it have become secondary, as production methods have proved that we can almost always create a successful crop. Efficiency in harvesting and agricultural methods meant that we, helped by a bit of rain and sun, could create the necessary conditions for a successful harvest. To sum it up, you could say that weather prediction has gone from being utilitarian and concerned with ones physical survival to becoming a more conceptual, psychological practice. It implies a colonization of time – a colonization of the near future. I think weather prediction today has become a metaphor for the desire to control the weather. If it is foreseeable, it is also somehow manageable.

When you engage in and establish a relationship with your surroundings, it has consequences both for you and the surroundings. My interest is to focus attention on this sense of causality. Of course I am generalizing a bit, but the idea of "Double sunset", for instance, lies in the fact that it is clearly a construction – which may seem similar to the second world in *The Truman Show*. Actually, I do not think it is a parallel world, but a world inside our world.

This is an important difference. Perhaps one could say that Modernism, from which a general concept of space was developed, really focused on one-way communication instead of an exchange. The idea that the friction between you and your surroundings is a defining element of space was not cultivated until the late 1980s and 1990s through philosophers such as Deleuze, and with the reintroduction of phenomenology. This has opened up for a greater complexity in the notion of space. So I do not refer to the installations I create, including these artificially produced natural phenomena, as being outside or parallel to society. I would say they are microscopic engagements with and in society. And, what I think is maybe the most important aspect, they are *producers of reality*.

In the context of what you just said, regarding nature and society from this more general point of view, two opposing ideologies might be ascribed to exist defining man's relation towards nature. The first one, an ideological doctrine, refers to nature as a deterministic concept in which man is able to totally decipher its modes of production. The other is more physical or materialistic and regards man as being an adaptive part of the natural evolution. In philosophical terms, do you regard man as being a part of nature or above it?
Well, I find nature as such a very questionable concept. Every time we discuss nature we tend, more or less consciously, to introduce a hierarchy of what is beautiful, what is good, and so on. In our society, which still retains some of Modernism's ideals, we have not yet cultivated the polyphony with which we need to handle the notion of "nature". By polyphony I mean the fact that contradictory ideas about nature may coexist. If we did not embrace the complexity of nature, we would simply develop a new form of totality. In traditional artistic discussions one will encounter a history of nature that includes problematic concepts such as "Hohe Schönheit" and the sublime. Nature has been a carrier of symbolic or religious content. The concept should therefore be used with caution. Perhaps architecture has a more profound relationship with nature due to the environmental challenges that it has quite successfully dealt with during the last thousand years. The relation between object or building and nature differs from that between an artwork and nature.

In Latin, there exists the dialectic between *natura naturans*, the producing nature, and *natura naturata*, the produced nature. Throughout the history of art, foremost painting and sculpture rather copied nature in its formal appearance, and architecture rather employed its principales of growth. Your work might be positioned at a border zone between art and architecture. What is your response to that?
I agree with you that I work in-between the two. But I actually do not find representation superficial. To me representation is real. I would argue that the representational aspect of the world is more real than the romantic idea of the real.

When recreating natural phenomena in nature or indoors, such as my waterfall, which consists of scaffolding, a hose, pump, and water, I can claim that it is as real as any waterfall – the ones in the Alps, for instance. It is falling water, while still being a representation.

To be honest, I am not all that interested in nature. I am interested in people, in how people perceive themselves and their surroundings; in what gives people a sense of identity, a sense of self, of responsibility, tolerance – I could go on like this. In order to investigate this I need a language. If we stick to the term nature – which I have always been slightly sceptical about – it may be understood as a very open language that allows for great individual inter- pretation. To put it simply: I use nature as a language to express the things about people that interest me. When I do a rainbow in a garage, it is not that rainbows fascinate me particularly. I am interested in what the experience of the ephemerality of the rainbow does to you. For me natural phenomena may instigate a re-evaluation of the ideas we have about ourselves – which I find very exciting.

In relation to the creative will of the artist, you frequently described the observer as being creative too. In a certain way he or she finishes the work. I have always emphasized the importance of the spectator, the user, or the participant in my work – they are central elements. There are a few reasons for this. First of all one has to recognize that the communicative history of art – I mean the communication of art in museums and elsewhere, the rules regard- ing the art object and the user, has been very rigid. One of the first things that struck me when I started working with art was how organized the art system was. There were specific ways of perceiving, experiencing, and handling art. I then quickly became involved in discussions of performativity. Instead of looking at artworks as objects, as Modernity had suggested, we considered the performative aspect of the cultural context in which this object was experi- enced. The dematerialization of objecthood in art thus became a political issue and an institutional challenge. So dematerialization is not a formal act – it is a socio-political or even geopolitical action. It is not about making new rules, but rather about understanding that rules are constantly being renegotiated. In one situation we might well be able to use the existent practice of display- ing an object in a glass case in a traditional museum. But that very same object might in a different context require a completely different ideology of display. This brings me to the issue of the observer again, a term I actually do not use very often, because it implies passivity. Institutional systems such as art muse- ums often consider their visitors to be observers. I, of course, prefer to think about the visitor as a *producer*. If you produce your own reality, you also have to consider your responsibility in doing so. If you simply observe the world, you appear to be less responsible, because the world just flies by you.

Forcing the viewer to shift the focus of his experience from the object to the action itself, only his own relative, subjective perception seems of importance. Could you explain what importance "movement" in general has in your work?
Movement has not been a central issue in art and architecture history. I find that time is the key to our engagement with space as it gives everything else a degree of relativity. There is a far-reaching economy organized around non-relative objects today. Take the car industry, for instance: it has always emphasized the importance of presenting its cars as being of universal quality and timeless design. It tries to establish a non-negotiable idea of the object.

Let us return to Bregenz now. Calling the show "The mediated motion", I first of all wanted to focus on the fact that it is mediated, a representation. This is an important issue, because Zumthor seems to have a rather ambiguous relationship with what is real and what is not. One could say that he sometimes eliminates temporality. However, at times he is not wrong and he does introduce arguments that I find very healthy for spatial theory today. In "The mediated motion" time is a producer of the exhibition and its reality. Your movement through the show becomes the way you mediate and create it. I saw this bus full of architectural students visit the museum: they walked into Zumthor's space and moved about in a very strict manner, like in a coordinate system. They did not perceive the temporality that I actually think Zumthor has put into the building by distributing staircases and columns in a specific way.

Your sculptures and installations don't appear as "beautiful" objects in a classical manner, but rather as the "strangely" looking results of your staging processes. Do you regard your creations as art objects or as scientific machines to produce certain poetical effects?
Well, obviously I consider my objects as artworks, as I am an artist, not a scientist. I would not call the spaces I do architecture. They are artworks. But this does not mean that I cannot engage in scientific experiments or an architectural practice – I simply do it from the viewpoint of an artist. Actually the question, whether something is art or not has become obsolete, because no qualities are added to an object by calling it art. The reality production that is connected to a certain art machinery is not as dependent on the term "art" as it was thirty or forty years ago. In that sense I am rather relaxed about whether something is art or not. But I do think that artistic research and content, art as a socio-critical endeavour, is being marginalized even though the art market today is stronger than ever. It is therefore extremely important that art claims its territory.

Your exhibitions have been shown in some of the most iconic museums in Europe. Considering the interaction of art and architecture, is it inspiring for you to work in such places and do you react specifically towards them?
I typically prefer museums whose architects have created a signature, even though this signature may sometimes be counterproductive to the art being exhibited. Often my interventions take on architectural dimensions. Sometimes my work consists of simply adding an extra wall with a hole in it, through which light is emitted into a space, or the cutting of a hole in an already existent wall or ceiling. As we have already discussed, spaces are made up of various elements and relations. When I enter any kind of space, a museum for instance, there is no direct boundary between what I do, what the architect has done, what I think, what the architect has been thinking, what the curator thinks, what the director is thinking, what the audience is thinking, and what the people in the restaurant selling sandwiches to the people visiting my show are thinking. I try to emphasize this holistic approach in order to avoid giving the object the status of an icon.

The mediated motion, 2001, in collaboration with Günther Vogt, Kunsthaus Bregenz, 2001.

"Your movement through the show becomes the way you mediate and create it."

The weather project, 2003, The Unilever Series, Turbine Hall, Tate Modern, London, 2003.

"There is no direct boundary between what I do, what the architect has done, what I think, what the architect has been thinking, what the curator thinks, what the director is thinking, what the audience is thinking, and what the people in the restaurant selling sandwiches to the people visiting my show are thinking."

"I prefer to think about the visitor as a producer. If you produce your own reality, you also have to consider your responsibility in doing so."

"*Actually the question, whether something is art or not has become obsolete, because no qualities are added to an object by calling it art.*"

Double sunset, 1999, Utrecht, 1999.

"What I would like to suggest is that an exhibition includes the whole environment in which it takes place."

ORDINARY BEAUTY

Conversation between Peter St.John and Alice Hucker

Fig.1: *Brick House*, Roof Variations, London, 2001-5.

"I guess we are interested in reality and so we tend to search quite hard within each context to find specific things to work with."

When I look at your work I find a large variety of architectural expressions, yet no overall handwriting. How important is the context in your work? What influence does the actual situation have?

I like the fact that there is a variety and a lack of consistency in the way our works are conceived. I would say that we try to make convincing places as much as we make objects. To us the context is our starting point, and it does not really matter whether it is a fascinating context or a very ordinary one. Sometimes even its ordinariness can become a theme. I guess we are interested in reality and so we tend to search quite hard within each context to find specific things to work with. We examine and turn them over in our minds endlessly. Eventually we find a theme for the project within those circumstances. It gives it a kind of a natural strength within the context.

In your first monography published in 2002 (Knitting Weaving Wrapping Pressing) you talk about your engagement with these found circumstances and your attempt to turn them into something new, yet well connected with the old, by distortion. Can you give us an example of this *as found* strategy in your work?

I think I could give you many. But the obvious example is a house that we have just completed in Paddington, which is build out of brick. (Fig.1 & 3) In that project we had an amazing client, who was determined to build a new house in this particular part of London, because of its vitality and because it was convenient for their work. But it was a part of London, where there were no real sites for building houses any more. After a year of searching we found this plot of land, which was a former car mechanics garage. This site was, I think, in most people's minds completely unsuitable for a house. It was utterly concealed from the street, it had a very complicated shape, and it had an enormously difficult legal situation of boundaries with so many adjoining owners. But to us it was very interesting, as it seemed almost as if we are working with the last piece of land left in London. As you probably know, London has this organic structure, having grown together as a series of villages. As a result you will sometimes find oddly shaped pieces of land left at the edges of more rational development. While most people might find those situations unworkable, we worked on it until the difficulty of the site and the awkwardness of its shape became a theme. We made a house whose character was entirely about the interior character of the site being surrounded by buildings. We made a plan that took advantage of the strange complexity of the site with its pointed corners. So it was as if the adversity of the site was turned on its back and became the character.

Another strong connection to the context is your choice of material; for example brick as you just mentioned, which has a strong local tradition in London.

Yes, we are often using materials for reasons of resonance with the local circumstances, but never to make them more ordinary. Hopefully there is always a way of treating these conventional materials in an ambiguous and unexpected way. I like the fact that our buildings are a bit confusing – a little bit unsettling in that way. These materials are familiar, heavy and normally not associated with contemporary architecture, but the way we have used their weight and thickness brings with it an unusual, archaic atmosphere. It is about treading a careful line between conservatism and poetry.

Once I read an interesting comment by you: "We prefer characterful ugliness to calculated perfection." Can this be seen as an antagonism to the minimalist scene in London?

It is a counter-proposal to a number of themes in London. I suppose at the time we made that statement we were specifically talking about the local circumstances of London and the narrative of London architects. Until quite recently the so-called "High Tech" architects of London, Norman Foster and Richard Rogers, were the ones whose architectural language was thought to be most interesting. The themes in their kind of work have a long tradition in this country, which can be seen in the great engineering works of the Victorian architects, where technology generates a kind of architecture, which is beautiful in its own way – just like a piece of product design is beautiful without having very much to do with being part of a fabric of the city. We have our own counter-idea of London, which enjoys of its relaxed ordinariness and variety. London is a generous and tolerant city to live in, and its organic messiness is one reason for that. We have been trying to make work about that context, a more human and less idealistic view of the future of London. Now it is different. London has become more international over the last five years. There are more architects from other countries building in London than there used to be. We feel just as related to the architects on the continent as we do to British architects. Therefore it is not quite such a specific discussion as it was then.

We are also interested in the relation between architecture and the natural elements: fire, water, air and earth. How are the cosmic forces connected to your architecture?

Do we consciously work with the four elements? I have never thought of it like that. But I do think it is related to our view that architects make real objects, whose physical presence can have a powerful effect. In our work you will recognize a preference for construction as a kind of mineral assembly, where material and technique are used in a painterly way for its reaction to natural and artificial light-reflecting, absorbing and holding shadow. We spend a lot of time thinking about the life of a material and how it is made. Your question makes me think of bricks, which, as you know, come to life through extreme heat.

In the Brick House there is an idea of the warmth that is coming from the colour, but also from the evidence of heat in its vitrified surface. There was a lot of effort involved in the choice of that brick. I would say that our architecture is full of metaphors, because we are interested in the idea of communicating. So for me an ideal project is one that perhaps resonates and reminds you of many things and not just one. At Kalmar for example there were these amazing granite rocks on the square. (Fig.4) These are very characteristic stones that were used to make pavements in the 17th and 18th century. These stones were originally lifted from the fields to make walls in that part of Sweden, and were then taken from the walls to make pavements. So it was about a process of civilizing the landscape. Some of these stones have been carried 500 kilometres from glaciers in Norway. In that period of time they were mixed up and there was this glorious collection of bright minerals, which is very beautiful. Our project was about taking up the roads that have been laid on this square, reorganizing the material, but also keeping it to make a more consistent surface consisting of different kinds of stones organised according to their colour. Those things were always there, but the design made you more aware about them.

In your more recent projects there seems to be a tendency towards decoration. Where does this urge come from? Is there a formal aspect or connection to natural patterns?

I do not think it would be right to say that they have much to do with nature. It is more of a cultural interest in the history of using decoration in architecture. One has to say that Herzog & de Meuron have been experimenting with that idea long before we have. We have always been interested in the material effect of construction and decoration as another way of experimenting with surface. We have used this idea in two recent projects, but in both of them the use of decoration has arisen out of specific cultural contexts. Our project for the *Museum of Childhood* in Bethnal Green, which has an elevation made with a variety of coloured stones, is like that because it is an extension to a listed Victorian building from a period when decoration was freely used. (Fig.2) We were trying to give the building a decorative language, which perhaps the building never had, but might have wanted to have. So to me this is a contextual response. Similarly, I showed your students our project for an office building in King's Cross today, which has a deeply incised decorative pattern on the precast concrete elements that frame the elevations. The site is an extraordinary situation between two magnificent Victorian railway stations. The design is our response to that, but it is also an attempt to show how a masonry facade with depth and detail can be used on a commercial office building, which in London today tends to have non-descript, systematic, and glazed facades.

Fig.2: *Bethnal Green Museum of Childhood*, Front Elevation, London, 2003-06.

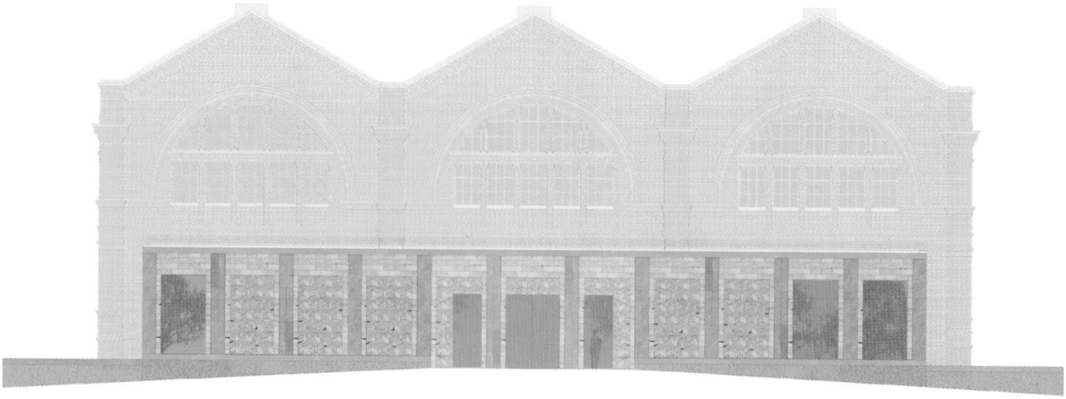

Many of your buildings have crystalline forms in their ground plans and/or sections. What are your general strategies regarding form? When does form emerge in your design process?

We are interested in form. We sketch and make models constantly. But form for us is not the important thing as it is for some architects. It is true that some of our buildings have a free and crystalline geometry, but it is usually a spatial idea generated from the interior rather than a formal idea about the external shape. Generally we try to avoid an architecture, where the form is the most powerful aspect of the building. I think that has a lot to do with our respect for the context. We try to make buildings, which engage with their circumstances rather than stand out. You will almost always find that our plans are simple and rectangular. We are avoiding a rhetorical architecture and look for a more slowly appreciated effect. It takes a bit more time to appreciate it and you might even miss it, but at least it does not make the world around it look out of date.

Many of your works are connected to the art scene. How do you collaborate with artists and how did this connection to the art scene develop?

We are interested in art and being in London we have always been able to go to galleries and exhibitions of contemporary art. From the beginning of our practice we built up connections with artist friends, which led eventually to the design of exhibitions and subsequently to building commissions for art institutions. We are working on a project with Damien Hirst, but the project is in an early stage, and could not yet be described as a collaboration. We have worked with a number of artists who have come to us, because they can see in our gallery work an understanding of the kind of environment required for the installation of their art. It is a careful judgement between a deference to the quiet circumstances that an artwork needs for its ideas to be heard and the specific character of the architecture.

At our chair we are quite interested in the aspect of globalism. How is your attitude towards global, generic movements vice versa local architecture?

I think it is important, but I do not like it. I am suspicious of architects operating well out of their contexts. Rem Koolhaas and others are adding fuel to the fire of these circumstances and are enjoying a certain lack of control. Our architecture comes from trying to do things slowly. It stems from collaborations and understanding specific contexts. To us this is a kind of resistance to the current pressure of constant invention and new output, something that has become almost independent from the reality of construction. We are very suspicious about that and not convinced that this is for the good.

Fig.3: *Brick House*, London, 2001-5.

Fig.4: *Kalmar Stortorget*, Sweden, 2000-3.

"Our architecture comes from trying to do things slowly."

THEORY, PRACTICE AND LANDSCAPE

Conversation between Stan Allen and Florian Sauter

"All architectural representation is fundamentally abstract. These disembodied and abstract means are actually the power of architecture."

**One sentence that struck me in your book *Practice* is a quotation by Dave
Hickey, which says architecture is a practice and not a science. In that perspective, how do you regard the terms of architectural theory and practice today?**
This is obviously a long-standing concern of mine. It is interesting that this
debate has also taken a curious turn recently with this whole discussion around
critical or *projective practice*. What are my responses to that debate? In one
sense you could say that projective practice is a tautology, because all practices
are projective. On the other hand you might say critical practice is a contradic-
tion in terms, because there exists an essential tension between critique, which
necessarily has to come from the outside, and practice that has to come from
the inside of the discipline. I think it is important to keep in mind two senses of
the word practice in this context. One is practice as the exercise of a discipline.
Hickey's sentence is provocative in that sense. He is reminding us that creative
practices are continuously redefining their own rules from the inside. With each
new circumstance encountered, the rules get revised and adjusted. In moments
of innovation or creativity the rules get rewritten and restructured in order
to drive the discipline forward. In one sense that is not unlike the best models
of scientific inquiry, which are also continually questioning their own models.
What I think he and I would both argue against is the idea that practice is simply the application of rules that are written down or created elsewhere. That is
where I think this potentially damaging split between theory and practice can
arise – the idea that there is some separate discourse called theory and that
practice is simply the application of those rules that are determined elsewhere.
The other sense of practice that is of significance to me is a collective one of
large numbers of individuals. When we talk about collective social practices
– the way in which people react to buildings and behave in the city – they are
again somewhat outside the control of the architect. Practice in that sense talks
about the collective creativity of individuals in the world outside the domain of
architecture. I think this to be an important factor to counterbalance the notion
of the individual creative practice.

**An important tool to link theory and practice together is the drawing. As Robin
Evans has succinctly put it, "architects do not make buildings, they make drawings for buildings". How do you regard the drawing as a translational medium?**
This is for me the fundamental paradox of architecture: I do believe that the
architect's job is to make buildings – it is this capacity to have a real effect and
to produce a concrete physical change in the city that distinguishes architecture
as a practice apart from say, art practices on the one hand, or social criticism
on the other. That is something which is architecture uniquely able to do. However
you have to recognize that you can only effectively accomplish that by working

through this disembodied abstract means, which is drawing or today's other various forms of representation. For me a lot of misunderstanding arises out of not recognizing that fact. In other words, to focus on drawing is not to say building is not important. It is to say that drawing has a very particular role within the process of imagining, visualizing, describing, testing and then ultimately realizing buildings. One of the key essays of Evans is called "Translations from Drawing to Building". He basically compares architecture to other art forms, for example sculpture or painting, where the artist has direct contact with the material. He says that it is often seen for architecture to be a liability that architects do not have that direct contact with the material. He concludes that maybe if architects would build their work more directly you would have a better architecture, but you would also have a *smaller* architecture. That is to say you can never imagine the architect building anything larger than a single family house. Architecture would lose its social and political power to intervene in the larger collective of the city. This again is accomplished through other forms of representation. I am in total agreement with Evans' idea that these disembodied and abstract means are actually the power of architecture. It is an asset and not a liability.

What is your personal approach towards the drawing as an instrument to visulize the concrete spaces?

I am in this sense somewhat old-fashioned and probably marked by my education particularly at the Cooper Union with John Hejduk. For example at the Cooper Union in the early 1980s we were forbidden to draw perspectives. Perspectives to Hejduk were pictorial, fake, and illusionist. He insisted on the axonometric, which was precise, measurable and leading towards construction. It is interesting, because the whole discussion has been lost a little bit today since it is so easy to make perspectives on the computer. I would like to say two things on that regard: one is I still have a kind of strong believe in the precision of the plan and the kind of verifiability of the axonometric. But I am also aware, like any architect working today, that all of that has to be discussed in the context of the computer. For me the difference is that with conventional drawings you construct and imagine a three-dimensional object out of a series of two-dimensional drawings. Today we tend to work directly through three-dimensional computer modelings and than produce the two-dimensional out of the three-dimensional. There has been a real inversion in that regard. Even though we are modeling on the computer in my office, I still like to see everything drawn out and turned into line drawing. The key characteristics of the architectural drawing are measurability and linearity, the potential of the line to describe a profile. Although we operate now under a different technological regime, some of those aspects still have a conceptual power.

Remaining in the digital realm, I would like to ask you about the term index. They way I comprehend it is closely related to Wolf Prix's formulation of the *frozen chance*. How has the notion of the index been changed with the implementation of computer technologies, in which total memory and endless mutations seem possible?

It is a good question and I have three somewhat unrelated thoughts here. One is precisely as you would think that the computer would move people away from a kind of indexical operation, which is very much about imprints and traces. Nevertheless so many computer driven work does seem to start from a more or less fixed geometric scheme and then introduces distortions or variations. In that sense there is still this idea of constructing a design process, even though it is much more extended, fluent and rapid today. The second thing is really to resist what I would call the ideology of visualization – the use of the computer to simulate the appearance of the building with the notion that being able to see what the thing looks like on the screen will actually enable us to design more appropriately. That to me is to miss the point again that the architectural drawing and all architectural representation is fundamentally abstract. First of all you have to point out that a computer rendering is not actually simulating the appearance of the building. It is in fact simulating the appearance of a photograph of the building. What you are simulating is another form of representation and it is not the building in itself. The third point, which of course is where the computer has had a serious effect, is in fabrication itself. Rethinking the whole regime of working drawings enables the architect to actually be much closer to the act of fabrication today, because he or she controls the computer forms of production. You can bypass the contractor working drawings through the use of digital fabrication. It is in those areas where design and construction technology start to intersect and I see a great potential in the entire question of building-information-modeling.

What importance have physical models in your work?

Both in my teaching engagement and practice physical models are incredibly important, even though I have not necessarily written about them yet. I actually think that they are even more important since the emergence of the computer, partly because we tend to use laser cutters, milling and rapid prototyping machines to produce models now. There is already a kind of back and forth between the digital and the physical there. Physical models combine in a very powerful way a necessary element of abstraction. They are different in materiality and scale than the actual building, yet they have some of its object, physical and spatial quality. They still force you to imagine, but you are imagining on the basis of something that is three-dimensional to three-dimensional versus three-dimensional to two-dimensional.

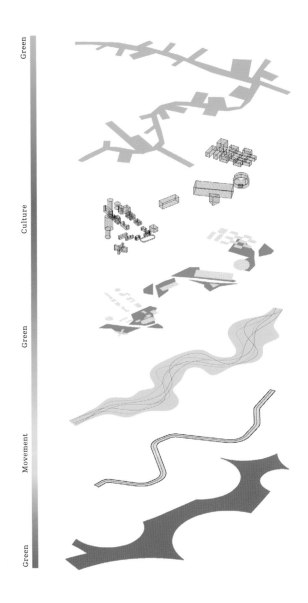

"Ecological thinking must be ecological – to think ecologically is to think about fluent, adaptive systems that incorporate feedback and change."

**You have been engaged with landscape projects for a long period of time
and your office "Field Operations" was concentrated around that topic.
Looking at it from an American perspective, is it something unusual to do?**
It is somewhat new to the degree that you could speak about a kind of emerging
discipline of what has come to be known as *Landscape Urbanism*. The key figures
there are Charles Waldheim and my former partner Jim Corner. I think there is
an emerging interest and focus that came out of a sense that landscape architecture was very well positioned to become a kind of synthetic discipline among
all the different disciplines that might contribute to a more holistic approach to
urbanism. That would include questions of ecology, and in this country very often
and presumably in Europe as well, dealing with problems of contaminated sites.
Landscape urbanism would find ways to integrate questions of infrastructure
and ultimately questions of architecture as well. It became a kind of "umbrella"
discipline, where you could incorporate all these different engineering, technical and architectural questions. My own particular history was in the beginning,
during the 1980s and the early 1990s, primarily concerned around questions of
representation and practice. Then during the period of the late 1990s I moved
into doing larger scale projects and developed that collaboration with Corner.
I became very interested in the relationship between architecture and landscape:
both urbanism and architecture could learn from landscape in not necessarily imitating landscape forms, but really thinking about landscape in terms of
process and change over time. Those were the elements that began to interest me
and it was formulized in the partnership with Corner. We did a number of competitions together and managed to win a couple. One of them was implemented.
We have subsequently separated our practices, but I continue to be interested
in large-scale work that is informed by landscape. Part of what led us to go separate directions is that Corner is more particularly a landscape architect and I am
more interested in the way in which landscape principals can be applied to architecture and urbanism. I would not identify myself as a landscape architect.

**Do you see in the landscape urbanism movement a possibility to regain a sort of
power to structure our environments, as opposed to simply erecting beautiful
and iconic objects that are functioning along corporate market conditions?**
Absolutely. I think that it inserts architecture into questions of infrastructure and
the construction of the site itself. It blurs the boundary between the object and the
field. All of these aspects I think are here to say that there is a very broad category
of architecture that is not per se a building. That could be surfaces, roads, infrastructure, and constructions in the site. For example one of the last projects that
Corner and I did together was a botanical garden for the University of Puerto Rico.

One of the things we agreed on the very beginning of the project with the client is that the site did not need more enclosed, air-conditioned buildings. Still we said there is going to be a very strong architectural component to this site that would include platforms, pavilions, canopies, amphitheaters, and market roofs. There is a whole series of very specific architectural interventions, but not one of them had a kind of enclosed envelope or designated interior and exterior distinction. For me that has become a very interesting area of investigation.

You already used the term ecology. With the idea of adaptation in mind, your concepts remind me of Charles Darwin's evolutionary theories. How do you react to such a reading of your work?
Well, this is the thing that initially drew me to the entire discussion around landscape. It was the landscape architects who were thinking about change and adaptation over time. It was very clear to me that certainly in the urban realm this is an absolute key issue and potentially in architecture as well, by switching our focus from the sort of perfect state of a building when it is initially finished to the life of a building, a city or an urban site over time. In general I would say less Darwin, but more Gregory Bateson. There is an aphorism by Bateson, which says, "Ecological thinking must be ecological". It sounds at first very tautological. What it means is that in many instances to think ecologically is to think about fluent, adaptive systems that incorporate feedback and change. Somewhere else Bateson talks about survival not in resisting change, but in terms of accommodating change. It means that your thinking has to be every bit as fluent and adaptive as the kinds of systems that you are talking about. In other words you can not apply rigid or dogmatic principals to systems that are themselves fluent, adaptable, changing and always incorporating feedback. As much as anything else it is not about a specific formal language and it is not necessarily about the presence of plants or green stuff in the building. It is a way of thinking that mirrors the dynamism of ecological systems themselves.

This question about ecology also leads us to a much more general scope of discussion. Looking at architectural history, it might be argued that Modernism was a very deterministic approach leading towards ideas of optimization, which were based on rationalistic principals from the 19th century. After the second World War the generic machine-metaphor was harshly criticised and a more specific approach to accept the local conditions was envisioned. For instance it is important to look at John Brinckerhoff Jackson's magazine "Landscape" here.
You are absolutely right. It does have a long history that sometimes people do ignore. Two key figures are J. B. Jackson and Ian McHarg. I think it has to

do with this more general sense of not imposing a system on either the people who will use the building or the site. You could almost say it is about creating a feedback loop between the site, the users and the architectural intervention. There was a certain belief animating early Modernism that was driven towards rationality and perfectibility. Of course, one of the things we know is that it was more a symbolic rationality than a real one. For example, if you look at the state of decay that many Modernist buildings are in you realize that time, which was less a variable for the Modernists, is always going to assert itself. Today one of the real changes is the idea that architects, landscape architects, ecologists and people thinking about the city are beginning to regard time as one of the important variables in architecture.

In a philosophical sense, would you agree with me that a certain shift from placing man in control above nature towards a comprehension of man as being a part of nature has occurred and is still affecting us today?
One of the sort of benchmarks in this whole discussion about landscape is the 1983 *Parc de la Villette* competition, in particular both the entries by Bernard Tschumi and Rem Koolhaas. The radical claim of that architecture in 1983 was directed against the sense of pastoralism of the 19th century in saying this is a vision for a 21st century park – it is going to incorporate technology and above all it is understanding nature as a cultural concept. That was the radical claim in 1983: nature as cultural construct. I think today that has almost been turned around and it is no longer a very radical claim. It is no longer a radical claim to say that all nature is constructed nature and that there is no such thing as a primeval landscape. Man has always been intervening in nature. With the emergence of things like bioengineering and nanotechnologies you could really say that culture is more being driven by nature than nature is being driven by culture at this point. There is a kind of awareness that we have a lot to learn from nature: not in an idealized way by looking at it as a sort of wild thing out there, but by regarding it as a kind of system that calculates and regulates. If we can understand those mechanisms, we can also produce an architecture that is more responsive.

In response to what you just said, I was quite astonished being in New York's Central Park. There you see squirrels running around in front of the sky-scrapers and you continously ask yourself what is now real and what is fake. The idea as you indicated is old, but still fascinating.
One of the things we learned from Bateson is that he understands ecology as information exchange. He is essentially applying a kind of cybernetic model to natural ecologies. This seems to me very powerful for a number of reasons:

first of all it does not idealize natural ecology as opposed to social ecology or any other kind of ecology. In other words you can understand all of them as systems of information exchange. For example if you look at Central Park: it is a landscape that has a certain amount of imbedded information. That imbedded information could be comprehended from the fact that the traffic is separated at different levels or that there is a way the people have of using it with big open spaces that provoke one kind of activity and dense landscapes that provoke another idea of activity. You can separate Central Park from its sort of cultural or historical context and then you can understand what works about it. The brilliance of Central Park arises from his continued usability. I mean here is a landscape that was designed in the middle of the 19th century for a whole set of both social expectations and technologies that have totally changed by now. In the 19th century people were meant to kind of stroll quietly through Central Park, the women in long dresses or on carriages. Those very same carriageways work really well for people on rollerblades or 21st century titanium racing bicycles. One of the reasons that Central Park has survived is that Olmsted understood that if it was too specific and too tight to those technologies it would become obsolete quickly, yet if it was too open and too general it would also die, because it would not have enough information and energy to carry it forward. Olmsted hit that dynamic just right: there is enough information to keep the system alive, but not too much to overdeterminate the uses.

Can we look at the ecological debate as a global movement that might be comparable to the International Style, even though it has no formal coherences? Or do we rather have to look at it in a sociological sense as just the outburst and most obvious result of a much wider cultural problematic?
There is certainly an emerging concensus; I have to say I am somewhat suspicious of the green solutions that are primarily technical. For me, the most urgent place to rethink architecture and ecology is in the urban realm. Its not enough to work building by building. So there is a lot of work still to do in this broad area of what could be landscape urbanism. That is a strategic question, and it intersects with policy and politics. On the other hand, I think we need to be more creative, and perhaps tactical within our own field. I like Alex Wall's suggestion of a "dirty" sustainability – low cost, hand's on solutions, rather than a kind of high tech answer. Iñaki Ábalos has pointed out that ecology and economy share a common origin. To build sensibly, with an economy of means, may be the best contribution to global sustainability.

Site Plan, *Taichung Central Parkway*, Taiwan.

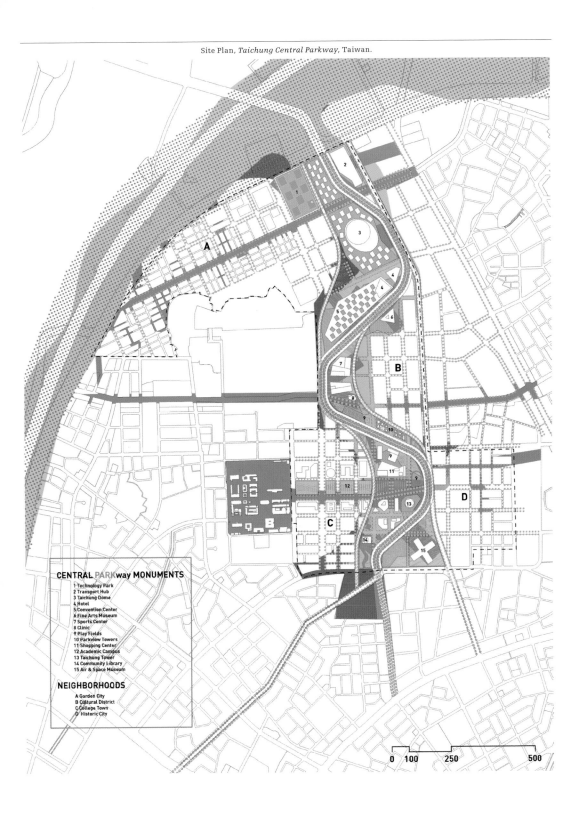

CENTRAL PARKway MONUMENTS
1 Technology Park
2 Transport Hub
3 Taichung Dome
4 Hotel
5 Convention Center
6 Fine Arts Museum
7 Sports Center
8 Clinic
9 Play Fields
10 Parkview Towers
11 Shopping Center
12 Academic Campus
13 Taichung Tower
14 Community Library
15 Air & Space Museum

NEIGHBORHOODS
A Garden City
B Cultural District
C College Town
D Historic City

0   100   250   500

WE ARE NATURE

Excerpt from a conversation between Paulo Mendes da Rocha and Florian Sauter
that took place in Zurich, 21 March 2007.

Mendes da Rocha House, Sao Paulo, 1960.

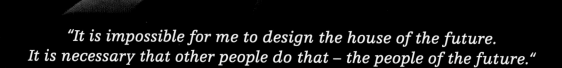

*"It is impossible for me to design the house of the future.
It is necessary that other people do that – the people of the future."*

To me a house is first of all a part of the city. A city needs to accommodate everybody at all times. The gratification of this elementary human necessity is the reason for every house's existence. In this sense the term "house" is a construction and "home" refers to a situation. Simultaneously man has in his creations tried to erect symbols. Always there has existed an interrelation between human needs for representation and survival. What we understand as symbolism is always connected to the historical comprehension of our own times. It is impossible for me to design the house of the future. It is necessary that other people do that – the people of the future. Today's life has nothing to do with the life in the Middle Ages. Just look at a Gothic cathedral: the individual stones were attached to each other without plaster. In comparison, today's reinforced concrete is completely different. I recently participated in an international congress in Napa Valley. The title of the symposium was curious: "Béton Armé – The Liquid Stone".

Returning to the primordial condition, I believe it is an eternal human wish to resolve gravity. In reality, buildings do not rest on the ground. Without the foundations everything would vanish. What actually carries the weight is in a precise and measurable relation to gravity. Envision the world in rotation for an instant. At a certain moment during that process a building might be facing downwards. One needs to be cautious about how the concept of buttressing a building occurs in reality. In my project for the Brazilian Pavilion at the Expo in 1970, you can clearly recognize that fact – it is liberated and open. Extinct by now, only photographs remain. Nevertheless it is alive in our memory. Architecture in this sense is a language and it is my means of expression and communication.

In general I think we constantly live in open spatial networks. You cannot proclaim a space to be democratic though, because we, the people, are the democracy. Imagine once a situation, where there are no more apartments available. If we would then take an immense prison and unlock all the latticed doors, spatial opportunities to inhabit would emerge. The activity can be democratic, but not the space. A poet, who was in jail once, said he felt free independent of his circumstances. Freedom for him existed in a psychological realm independent of a concrete spatial setting. The Brazilian Sculpture Museum I built has no doors or locks. The necessity to confine an artwork is the owner's longing for protection, because he has paid a considerable amount of money and consequently longs for security. The art works do not need any protection. In my opinion, the *Guernica* by Pablo Picasso should be exhibited freely in the airport of Madrid.

In response to the question whether man is in a modern sense positioned above nature – as dominating and in control – or in a postmodern perspective a part of it, I would like to suggest the following: imagine a human being 200000 years ago. Probably that creature washed his face with clean and clear water at the bank of a river. Now envision me washing my face this morning: the water came through a pipe. You can do whatever you want with nature. Nature alone, without human interventions, is preposterous. To use a further example to illuminate my standpoint, picture yourself as an astronaut, who watches the earth from outer space. Everything is dark. What you will see is the brightly lit cities. You might even announce that the planet emits its own light. It is simple: we are nature.

Sections of the *Expo Pavilion*, Osaka, 1970 .

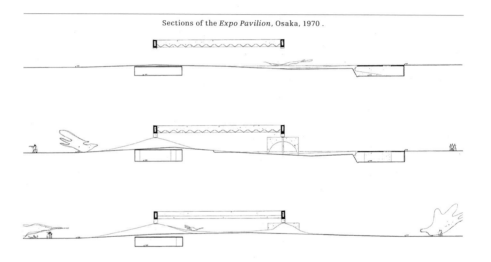

"In reality, buildings do not rest on the ground.
Without the foundations everything would vanish."

Expo Pavilion, Osaka, 1970 .

Brazilian Sculpture Museum, Sao Paulo, 1988.

*"You cannot proclaim a space to be democratic,
because we, the people, are the democracy."*

Site Plan, *Montevideo Bay*, 1998.

LOCAL AND GLOBAL

Conversation with Manuel Castells

The questions were prepared by Florian Sauter and Christian Schmid,
who is lecturing in sociology at the department of architecture at ETH Zurich.

Vis-à-vis the virtual realms of the Information Age, architecture is one of the last activities to manifest the fundamentally real – it gives meaning to the archaic and obvious, the world of sensations and the primary contact with the cosmos. How is the local connected with the global today and in what direction do you see the internet as the backbone of our global society emerging?

First, let me be clear that I am a researcher and therefore I only analyze and theorize what I observe, so I know nothing about the future, and do not predict anything. In terms of what I have been working on for years, I identified two con-tradictory trends in spatial forms and processes. On the one hand, the *space of places*, based on physical contiguity, continues to play a major role in constructing life and culture: it bounds our experience. On the other hand, the prevalence of global/local networks of digital communication as the backbone of our organizations, economy, media, political and social interaction, has cre-ated new forms of spatial relationships that I characterize as the *space of flows*. This simply means that the organization of simultaneity of shared practices (the function of the space of places) can be performed at distance by networks of instant interaction. When we say globalization, this is not that the whole world is the same country. It is that all essential activities are peformed in global networks that connect people and activities at distance. But the space of flows is not an abstraction: it results from the combination of various places that are linked in these networks. Flows circulate between these places and they receive their meaning and their function from the flows that circulate beween them. So, the space of flows comprises: specific places, systems of communication and transportation, and flows (of information, of people, of merchandise) that constantly circulate in these systems of communication. For instance the global city is not one particular city, e.g. New York or Zurich that has global financial or managerial functions. Most of London or most of Zurich is very local, not global. What is global (in terms of financial networks) is the assembling of specific places (the financial district and its ancillary functions and activities) in each city, and their connection in a global network of interaction. The internet, and other computer networks, including wireless communication provide the backbone for all essential activities in our societies and economies. But space does not disappear in a world of flows. It becomes shaped and specified in the new socio-technical structure.

| In what ways is the contemporary "reality" of architecture influenced by the "immateriality" of the new informational potentials?

Information is not inmaterial. To become communication, and therefore, produce an effect, requires physical places, major infrastructures, and commmunication channels. The design and production of spatial forms and processes is the domain of architecture. Thus architecture not only continues, but becomes essential, because it must provide the functional and cultural bridge between places and flows. This is increasingly so in the era of mobile communication that makes the use of Internet and other digital transmission systems ubiquituous. Thus, we move to a hybrid space, as William Mitchell has brilliantly theorized, in which communication networks are folded in physical places, and these places receive meaning as multifunctional nodes of communication networks. Instead of "smart buildings", what we have now is "communicative cities".

Would you agree with me that architecture has discovered new possibilities to actively engage in the contemporary media spectacle?
What further consequences do you recognize in these processes?

Architecture oscillates between *reinventing monumentality* (the iconic building or bridge or museum) and *reconstructing culture* in the space of flows by providing meaning to public spaces, be it squares, stations and airports. In both cases, it fights against the uniformity of mass produced space and asserts the significance of spatial forms. *It is not spectacle, it is meaning through form within function.*

What kind of urban consequences does the information age bring with itself for our cities? Why do certain businesses still rely on a concrete need of physical adjacency?

One of the biggest myths is that information and communication technologies disolve urban concentrations. It is exactly the contrary. We have had in the last two decades the largest wave of urbanization in history, and it will continue. We are over 50% of urban population in the planet, and the projections are to reach 65% by 2030 and 75% by 2050. However, what has changed is the forms of urbanization. The urban form of the information age is the metropolitan region, large multifunctional expanses that connect several metropolitan areas along fast transportation lines and are interconnected around the world by telecommunications, internet and air transportation. This is the dominant process in all continents, including Europe as empirically shown by Peter Hall in his recent study on the *polycentric metropolis*. We have spatial concentration and metropolitan decentralization, precisely because ICT allows the simultaneous centralization and decentralization of activities and residences.

Thinking of architecture in political terms, how can it be used to balance the global inequalities, especially in regard to the dramatic developments of large urban slum areas? Adapting architecture to the needs of the people in each particular context, recognizing the value of traditional architecture, and helping the slums to be better built, safer and also more beautiful, because slums are increasing, not decreasing as urbanization increases faster than people's income.

How would you ask today's social question?
What are in your opinion the next steps that
have to be taken in order to develop a more
convincing idea of sustainability?

I am a researcher, not an ideologue, and I never
say what must be done. However, I can see that
people all over the world are increasingly critical of a civilization that has extraordinary technological and cultural potential and yet sees the
persistence of poverty for half of humankind,
together with increasing inequality, and dan-
gerous environmental deterioration that may
threaten the survival of our species (not of the
planet, of us in the planet). In this sense the
global movement against corporate globalization
has been an important voice to activate a necessary debate about our current model of growth
and social organization. Architects and planners,
as experts in the spatial forms of livelihood, have
a major role in influencing the debate. This is
indeed a political debate, but can be and must
be informed by analysis and alternative design.

FOUND PAPERS

10

ASSERTIONS ON ARCHITECTURE AND SCIENCE

by Marcel Meili

The following 10 assertions were presented at the colloquium "Umbildung 4" that was
organized by Prof. Dr. Akos Moravansky at ETH Zurich, 13 November 2006.

1. Architecture is genuinely a dialogic and discursive discipline. Theory (which means language about architecture) is therefore an indispensable component of the profession.

2. The architectural project, in the best case, is not only experience of reality, but also production of insights about reality. In this sense the project is a medium for the exploration of the world.

3. The theoretical discourse behind the production of a project is constitution-ally different from the critical, historical or scientific-observing discourse, which is applied to architecture from the outside. In a certain respect, both forms of discourse are even conversely structured.

4. The theoretical reflection that accompanies the project is directed towards productivity in design research. Its purpose is to open up conceptual fields of action for the design work and to make conjectures about possibilities, capacities or meanings.

5. The terminology and sentence-structure of theoretical positions accompa-nying design therefore have to oppose the traditional demands of "scientific rigour". The fuzziness of terms, the speculative, tentative and vague character of these – the preliminary unassessability of programmatic or theoretical prop-ositions are not weaknesses, but a specific feature of sentences which strive to create room for movement in another medium, which is drawing.

5a. This applies also to the architectural dialogue with other disciplines.

6. The theoretical discourse of architects is thus not an explanation of the project, but an integral part of it.

7. The theoretical discourse about architecture is subject to other scientific requirements. Critical-theoretical or historical research on architecture does not have the task of opening up fields of action; it rather orders, explains, creates categories and references, interprets, assesses and evaluates in a comprehensible manner. This is also, of course, production of insight.

8. These two forms of insight and knowledge-production do not develop inde-pendently of one another, they are two different forms of theory within the same gravitational field.

9. The question as to whether the theoretical code of the architect-designer is "scientific" or not, is less of a problem of architecture than a problem of the human sciences and institutions surrounding them, as well as of their scientific concept.

10. The *Urban Portrait of Switzerland* lays claim in no line to the status of "scientific rigour", but most certainly to that of – also theoretical – production of insight. Above all, the book lays claim to the status of a project.

"I WOULD PREFER NOT TO "

by Iñaki Ábalos

This article was originally published as "Bartleby, the Architect"
in the newspaper *El Pais*, 10 March 2007.

Project by Lacaton & Vassal, *Léon Aucoc Square*, Bordeaux, 1996.

Every ten years or so, architects come under the attack of a magical word. Many succumb to its spell, but nobody is entirely free of its effects on their way of working. Even as the last notes of the song of "intelligent" buildings can still be heard, so "sustainability" as the quintessence of architecture has begun to sweep through everyday language. There is now no chair of urban development in any council, who does not systematically demand irreproachable sustainability – with no impact on the budget and without sending the city-business model into crisis, of course. Architects now feel obliged to embark on a delicate mission and are helping to pad the word out with spurious meanings to the extent that eventually, between them, they will drain it of all significance.

In parallel to these semantic abuses, the approval of the *Technical Building Code*[1] has resulted in major changes to construction practices and a considerable effort in regards to the collaborative technique of architects and their consultants. They are obliged, if they wish to go beyond strict convention, to rethink the very way that they work, and are forced to replace the "constructive experience" with environmental models. These parameters bring physicists, environmentalists and engineers into the design process, just as specialists in structure and installation calculations appeared on the scene some years ago.

This shift from the mechanical to the energetic in the choir of experts, who accompany the solo voice of old architects, clearly reveals the abandonment of a Modern concept of architecture based on modular mass production and industrial materials for a concept that some authorities, among them Sanford Kwinter, have been quick to dub "thermodynamic". Thermodynamic stands as a description of the rejection of the "tectonic" model of traditional knowledge (and teaching) of architecture and its replacement with a new "biotechnical" concept/teaching. This is capable of equipping the architect with the tools to view his buildings as *living beings*, which are as entities engaged in a permanent interchange of energy with their surroundings and endowed with a limited lifecycle. Despite the somewhat messianic tone of this idea, a certain unanimity has built up around it in academic circles at least – not just in Spain, as demonstrated by the more or less explicit advance of this idea in American universities, where possibly as being the last country to arrive at an environmental culture, it has an overwhelming effect today.

The problem arises as we begin to consider, what the big words and the good intentions end up with, when the voices in the choir become a noise that starts to drown out the soloist – a choir urged on by a construction industry that has at last identified *business* in the magical word. Despite the efforts made by a number of institutions in the sector, the impression conveyed at seminars, congresses and similar gatherings is that the examples presented are nothing but a parade of spectacular prostheses of technological gadgets, turning old

and bad buildings into high-tech drag queens more often than not.
The trivialisation of sustainability brought about by this pseudo-technical and marketing-based concept is as boring for architects and especially for students, as it is exciting for the big consultancy firms and politicians.

This situation has sounded alarm bells in various North American institutions of cultural importance and prestige (among them the *Canadian Centre for Architecture*, directed by Phyllis Lambert, and its *Study Centre*, directed by Mirko Zardini). Such institutions have decided to intervene and to foster serious debate, firstly with their international consultants and secondly in the form of seminars, books and exhibitions, all with the aim of exploring the true architectural and cultural nature of sustainability.

The central idea is simple: only if there is a real idea of beauty hidden among all this rhetoric, will it be possible for sustainability to mean anything and be something intended to stay. Architecture must refuse to bow before all the pomp and fuss. It should ask itself, what it is that is interesting about this notion and thereby introduce an aesthetic aspect into the debate. So far, one idea has resonated in the early debates among experts – the idea that it is *Bartleby*, the character created by Melville, with his famous phrase, "I would prefer not to", that best expresses the aesthetic dimension of sustainability by questioning the very need for action (an idea put forward years ago by Cedric Price, which, if put into practice with common sense, here and now, would have saved us the brutal colonisation of the Spanish coast over the last ten years).

Some might say that this kind of idea would be the suicide of architecture and would not result in its aesthetic renewal. There are, however, examples, such as the French studio Lacaton & Vassal that expose this as a lie. These architects, who trained in Africa – where ecology and economy mean survival – decided they "would prefer not to" when commissioned to improve *Place Léon Aucoc* in Bordeaux (1996), which locals liked and was already sufficiently developed. So instead, they allocated some of the budget to laying new gravel, repairing the benches and replacing the odd kerbstone. Why, they asked themselves, should it be necessary to do something spectacular? What had the citizens done to deserve such treatment?

The work they did was minimal, but the neighbours were overwhelmingly pleased, as are the artists invited now years later to exhibit their artworks in the *Palais de Tokyo* (2001). Also refurbished by Lacaton & Vassal, they left it practically bare, ready for action rather than finished in full make-up. As an aside, I invite anyone travelling to Paris to cross the Seine and to visit on the same day the Palais de Tokyo and the newly opened *Musée du Quai Branly*, where the signature of Jean Nouvel has been successful in generating queues of people wishing to view (or attempt to view) an interesting collection, but in which every single decision – be it formal or banal – and the profusion reveal a lack of understanding or indeed display obscene indifference to the cultures displayed.

It is no coincidence that sustainability's rejection of technological manipulation implies to attempt going back and starting from the beginning, restoring a certain naturalness or normality to the role of architecture and design in the city and everyday life. *Super Normal* is the term used by the designer Jasper Morrison, together with Naoto Fukasawa, to promote an environment of well-crafted objects in the world of design – which is unquestionably even more affected than architecture by the need for originality through its demand of showiness.

A credible map of sustainability has yet to be drawn, but there can be no doubt that other aspects already trailed and trialled have run out of whatever credibility they had. Bartleby the architect's time has come and the entire academic, as well as cultural apparatus supports him.

1 New Spanish law on the building standard.

DARWIN ON OUR DESK

by *Josep Lluís Mateo*

Excerpt from the text "Invocación a la Belleza" (Invocation of Beauty) that was published in *Textos Instrumentales*, Ed. Gustavo Gili, Barcelona, 2007 (Spanish) and *Josep Lluís Mateo*, Ed. Electa, Milan, 2007 (Italian).

Clockwise different birds from Charles Darwin's *Zoology of the Beagle*:
Otus Galapagoensis, Tanagra Darwini, Xanthornus Flaviceps, Milvago Albogularis.

The second argument refers to architecture as a physical construction that is consequently subject to the laws of science and matter. To explain the link between this physical world and beauty, I use what I call the **"organic metaphor"**, present implicitly or explicitly in the work of many architects as a conceptual structure or an adopted language.

From a Darwinian viewpoint that sees adaptation to the environment as the fundamental principle governing the form of a living being, the scientific and objectivist thinking of the 19th century came to understand the world and defend the assumption that **the natural phenomenon, the product of adaptation and of an internal logic associated with the functional needs of the organism, is beautiful.** The possibility of explaining the form of the object in terms of rational parameters renders it comprehensible, precise, inevitable and, therefore, beautiful.

A hippopotamus or a rhinoceros would, in consequence, be as beautiful as a horse, despite the fact that the horse is graceful, the hippopotamus ungainly and the rhinoceros archaic. Nonetheless, each of them can be understood according to the specific framework of needs and adaptations that have produced a given structure and the organization of its parts, from which none can be eliminated without affecting the balance of the others. As a result, these animals are not only comprehensible, but actually beautiful.

A **monster**, conversely, is a being that lacks this coherence: an artificial structure without the capacity to survive, an entelechy devoid of organic logic.

Just as this scientific approach breaks down every organism into a series of interrelated systems (the bones or structural system, the muscles, the arteries or system of fluids, the skin, etc.), a building can also be seen as a coherent framework of systems: if one part is eliminated (and this is confirmed by everyone, from Vitruvius to Mies van der Rohe), the organism collapses. The most developed beings, to continue with the metaphor, are those that generate the autonomy of their parts. A primitive organism, such as a formless amoeba, therefore develops in such a way as to provide itself with a structure, a hierarchy within the assemblage of the necessary parts. One of the first steps in a project consists in defining a structure as a system of hierarchical organization of the parts, distinguished from what is not structure, which is then superposed with the systems of internal fluids that regulate the different types of movement – of people, gases, etc. The statics of both the structure and the framework of movements are dynamic systems, systems of movements. Working with the structure means working with the movement of loads. Statics represents control of the dynamics of the loads, to which must be added the movement of fluids (persons, gases, liquids), lifts, stairs, and systems of ventilation. All of this involves a principle of structuring.

The **coherence** between interconnected parts, each operating normally, without hindrance due to these interrelations, is, then, from this viewpoint, the designer's objective, in which **beauty** is the product of the precision of the parts and the harmonious functioning of the whole.

ARCHITECTURE IS

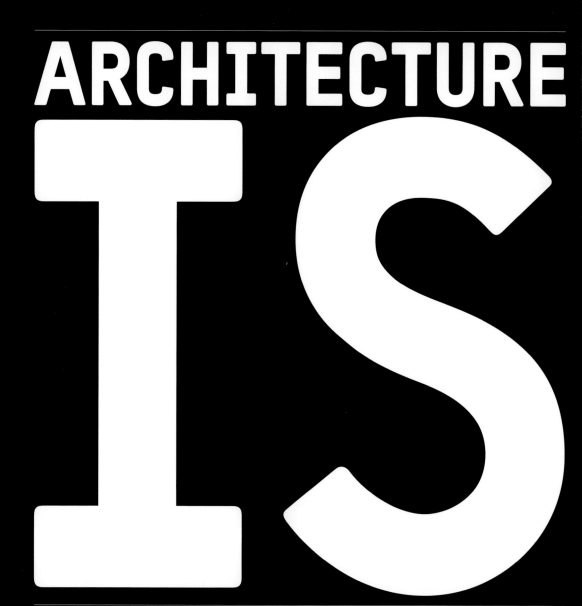

by Renzo Piano

The following article was originally published in *Ano*, Nr. 1 in 2007,
entitled "Reflexiones desde la Pontificia Universidad del Perú".

I see architecture as an adventure – an adventure in many respects. First of all, it is an adventure with regard to reality. When we erected a building in Japan, we had to cope with 38 earthquakes. We were forced to build under extreme conditions. With a building in New Caledonia we suffered a number of hurricanes. Believe me, dealing with winds of 250 kilometer an hour is a veritable adventure. Architecture is an adventure, because it is real – it is about making things and shaping pieces. It involves designing tools, digging deep into the rock and fighting against gravity.

But architecture is an adventure in another sense too – it is a quest into the spirit. An architect is comparable to an explorer like Robinson Crusoe: whenever you enter a new site, you must work with whatever you have at hand, otherwise you will fall into the trap of style. Style is a terrible thing. Style is like a gilded cage, a hallmark or a pain you recognise. Ultimately it is not very interesting, because a true explorer is free. Architecture is comparable to seeing in the dark. You know that if you look into the dark for long enough, after a while you begin to make out things that you would not be able to see if you did not peer at them obstinately.

Architecture deals with rebellion. It is a rebellion against convention. It is in fact a search for freedom from others and from oneself. Architecture is about utopia, and there is nothing to be said against utopia. I believe that if you do not have the spirit that derives from utopia, then you really should change your profession.

Lastly, I have to say that architecture is a spiritual adventure, because it is a highly complex profession. It is complicated, because it is a mirror of life. Life is complicated, but architecture is even more complicated. In all likelihood, architecture is the oldest profession in the world – by the virtue of being so old, it also behaves very instinctively.

Architecture is complicated too, because it is full of contradictions – for example the contradictions between freedom and discipline or between order and disorder. These are, however, contradictions within which the architect must survive and which he must accept. An architect needs discipline, but he also needs freedom. Only a fool would believe that he can opt for either one of them. The fact of the matter is that both are required. This ambiguity, this controversy, is essentially a part of the complexity of architecture.

Ansel Adams, *Clearing Winter Storm*, Yosemite National Park, 1944.

CONTRIBUTORS

IÑAKI ÁBALOS

Born 1956 in San Sebastian, Spain. Since 1984 he as worked together with Juan Herreros. They taught at the architecture school of Madrid between 1984 and 1988 and took part in numerous workshops and international seminars, among others at Columbia University, the Architectural Association and the EPFL in Lousanne. He is currently holding the Jean Labatut Professorship in Architecture at Princeton University.

Iñaki Ábalos and Juan Herreros have taken part in individual and collective exhibitions such as "Light Construction", "Groundswell", and "On Site" (MoMA, New York, 1995, 2005, 2006), as well as "New Trends in Architecture" and "Dialogue" (Tokyo, 2002, 2005). Their most recent solo exhibition "Grand Tour" was organized by ICO in Madrid. They are the authors of *Le Corbusier: Skyscrapers* (Madrid: 1987), *Natural-Artifical* (Madrid: 1999), *The Good Life* (Barcelona: 2001), *Tower and Office* (Cambridge: 2003) and *A Picturesque Atlas Vol.1&2* (Barcelona: 2005, 2006).

STAN ALLEN

He was educated at Brown University (BA, 1978), The Cooper Union (B.Arch, 1981) and Princeton University (M.Arch, 1988). After working for Richard Meier in New York and Rafael Moneo in Spain, he established his own office in 1990. From 1999-2003 he worked in collaboration with James Corner (*Field Operations*). The work of this interdisciplinary collaboration was recognized with first prizes in several invited competitions, for example the re-use of *Fresh Kills* in Staten Island (2001).

From 1989 to 2002 Stan Allen taught at Columbia University's Graduate School of Architecture, Planning and Preservation, where he was the Director of the Advanced Design Program. Since 2002 he is the Dean of the Architectural School in Princeton. His projects have been published in *Points and Lines: Diagrams and Projects for the City* (New York: 1999) and his theoretical essays in *Practice: Architecture, Technique and Representation* (Australia: 2000).

MANUEL CASTELLS

Born 1942 in La Mancha, Spain. He studied law and economics at the University of Barcelona between 1958 and 1962. He had to flee the country and finished his studies as a political refugee at the Sorbonne in 1964. After completing a doctorate in sociology at the University of Paris, he taught in Paris between 1967 and 1979, first at the Nanterre Campus and then at the Ecole des Hautes Etudes Sciences Sociales. In 1979 he was appointed professor of sociology and professor of city and regional planning at the University of California, Berkeley. In 2001 he became a research professor at the Universitat Oberta de Catalunya (UOC) in Barcelona. In 2003 he joined the University of Southern California (USC) Annenberg School of Communication as a professor.

Manuel Castells received numerous honorary doctorates and other honors in recognition of his work. Books written by him are *The Urban Question* (London:1977/1972), *The Informational City* (Oxford: 1989), and *The Network Society* (Center for Transatlantic Relations, 2006).

CATHERINE DUMONT D'AYOT

She studied architecture and conservation at the Institute of Architecture and Urbanism at the University of Geneva. Until 2005 she taught at the University of Geneva and since 2006 she has been teaching at the ETH in Zurich.

Catherine Dumont D'Ayot was the editor of the architectural magazine *FACES* until 2003. In 2006 she edited together with Bruno Reichlin the exhibition catalogue *Jean Prouvé: The Poetics of the Technical Object* for the *Vitra* Design Museum in Weil am Rhein.

OLAFUR ELIASSON

Born 1967 in Copenhagen, Denmark. He attended the Royal Academy of Arts in Copenhagen from 1989 to 1995. He has participated in numerous solo and group exhibitions worldwide and his work is represented in public and private collections, including the Solomon R. Guggenheim Museum, New York, the Museum of Contemporary Art, Los Angeles, the Deste Foundation, Athens, and the Tate Gallery, London. His major solo exhibitions were at Kunsthaus Bregenz ("The Mediated Motion", 2001), Musée d'Art Moderne de la Ville de Paris ("Chaque matin je me sens différent. Chaque soir je me sens le même", 2002) and ZKM Karlsruhe ("Surroundings Surrounded", 2001). He represented Denmark at the Biennale in Venice in 2003 ("The Blind Pavilion").

Olafur Eliasson works in Berlin and has founded together with his wife the charity foundation *121 Ethiopia*. The San Francisco Museum of Modern Art is currently organizing his first solo exhibition in the United States ("Take Your Time", 2007).

PATRICK GARTMANN

Born 1968 in Chur, Switzerland. He studied engineering and architecture at the University of Applied Sciences in Chur (HTW). After graduation in 1998 he was an assistant teacher at the chair of architecture and design of Valerio Olgiati at the ETH in Zurich. Between 2001 and 2005 he was a lecturer in information technology and basic principles of construction at the HTW in Chur. Since 2006 he has been a lecturer in the Master program at the technical University in Lucerne (HTA).

In practice Patrick Gartmann is collaborating with Jürg Conzett and Gianfranco Bronzini. Their work has received numerous awards. In 2006 the monograph *Structure as Space* was published on their work by the Architectural Association in London.

TONI GIRONÉS

Born 1965 in Badalona, Spain. In 1992 he received his architectural degree from ETSAV in Barcelona (Escola d'Arquitectura del Vallès). There he taught as associate professor until 2005. Since then he is the director of studies at the architecture school in Reus (Universitat Rovira i Virgili).

Toni Gironés has an independent professional practice since 1993. His work has been published widely in Spain and received a number of awards. He has lectured at different architectural schools, among others the University of Rosario, Santa Fe, Posadas, Palermo (Argentina), Ferrara (Italy), ETSAB, ESARQ and Ramon Llull. He is currently working on his doctoral thesis: "Spontaneous Architecture: Thoughts on architectural Constants" at the ETSAB in Barcelona.

ALICE HUCKER

Born 1975 in Ulm, Germany. She studied architecture at the ETH in Zurich. In 1998 she was an exchange student at the Technical University in Delft. After her graduation in 2002 she was employed in the office of Marcel Meili and Markus Peter. There she worked on the Hardturm Stadium in Zurich, as well as the competitions for Helvetia Patria in Milan (1st Prize) and the Triemlispital in Zurich.

Since 2005 Alice Hucker has been an assistant teacher at the chair of architecture and design of Josep Lluís Mateo at the ETH in Zurich.

MAI KOMURO

Born 1983 in Osaka, Japan. She did her Bachelor Studies in architecture and engineering at Kyoto University between 2001 and 2005. Since 2005 she is enrolled in her Master studies at the University of Tokyo in the laboratory of Manabu Chiba. Throughout the academic year 2006-7 she was an exchange student at the department of architecture at the ETH in Zurich and participated in the landscape laboratory of Josep Lluís Mateo and Christophe Girot.

In 2005 Mai Komuro received the "Goichi Takeda Award" (the first prize of the diploma projects at Kyoto University) and the Silver Prize at JIA National Competition of Graduating Students.

CHRISTIAN KEREZ

Born 1962 in Maracaibo, Venezuela. He was educated at the ETH in Zurich and graduated in 1988. He was a design architect in the office of Rudolf Fontana from 1991 to 1993. After extensively published work in the field of architectural photography, he opened his own architectural office in Zurich in 1993.

Christian Kerez has been a visiting professor at the ETH in Zurich since 2001 and has been appointed assistant professor in design and architecture. His work has been shown in solo exhibitions at the EPFL ("The Scales of Reality", 2006) and the Swiss Architecture Museum in Basel ("Interior Views", 2006). In 2007 he won the architectural competition for the Museum of Modern Art in Warsaw.

MICHAL KRZYWDZIAK

Born 1975 in Cracow, Poland. He studied civil engineering combined with marketing and management at the University of Technology in Cracow between 1995 and 2000. Afterwards he worked as a project manager for Landolt & Haller Architects in Zurich.

In 2004 Michal Krzywdziak started his architectural education at the ETH in Zurich and has recently completed the 3-year Bachelor program. In 2007 he was a student at the chair of architecture and design of Josep Lluís Mateo and took part in the housing laboratory "Paris – Boulogne Billancourt".

JONATHAN LIN

Since 2005 he has been a student at the National University of Singapore (NUS). He is currently pursuing a Bachelor of Arts in Architecture. In 2006 he was the co-leader of the design and construction of "Treetops" Istana pavilion. He was also a participant of the *Habitat for Humanity* (HFH) design and construction project for a community hall in Botokenceng Yogyakarta, Indonesia (2006).

JOSEP LLUÍS MATEO

Born 1949 in Barcelona, Spain. He graduated from the ETSAB in Barcelona and in 1994 received his doctorate ("Cum Laude") from the Polytechnic University of Catalonia. Between 1981 and 1990 he was chief editor of the magazine *Quaderns d'Arquitectura i Urbanisme*.

Josep Lluis Mateo has had an independent practice since 1974 and his architectural work has been widely published, exhibited and awarded. Since 2002 he has been professor of architecture and design at the ETH in Zürich.

PAULO MENDES DA ROCHA

Born 1928 in Vitoria, Brazil. He graduated in architecture and urbanism from the Universidade Presbiteriana Mackenzie College of Architecture in Sao Paulo in 1954. He began to teach architecture and urbanism at the University of Sao Paulo (FAU) in 1959. In 1970 he realized the Brazilian Pavilion for the EXPO in Osaka.

Paulo Mendes da Rocha participated at the 10th Documenta in Kassel (1997) in the segment "100 Days – 100 Guests". In 2000 he represented Brazil at the Biennale in Venice and was awarded the *Mies van der Rohe* prize. He was the second Brazilian after Oscar Niemeyer to receive the *Pritzker* architecture prize in 2006.

MARCEL MEILI

Born 1953 in Küsnacht, Switzerland. He studied at the ETH in Zurich between 1973 and 1980, among others with Aldo Rossi and Dolf Schnebli. Afterwards he was a scientific researcher at the institute for history and theory (gta) at the ETH in Zurich. Since 1984 he has been lecturing at various occasions, for example at the University of Applied Sciences and Arts in Zurich, the international summer academy in Berlin and Karlsruhe, as well as in Harvard. In 1987 he began his collaboration with Markus Peter. Many of his projects have been developed in cooperation with other offices, i.e. Fickert & Knapkiewicz, Miroslav Sik, Roger Diener and Herzog & de Meuron.

Since 1999 Marcel Meili is a professor for architecture and design at the ETH in Zurich. Together with Roger Diener, Jacques Herzog and Pierre de Meuron he is directing the ETH Studio Basel, which in 2006 published "Switzerland – An Urban Portrait".

RENZO PIANO

Born 1937 in Genoa, Italy. He graduated from the school of architecture at Milan Polytechnic in 1964. He subsequently worked with his father and later under the design guidance of Franco Albini. Between 1965 and 1970 he worked with Louis I. Kahn in Philadelphia and Z.S. Macowsky in London. His collaboration with Richard Rogers dates from 1971 (Piano & Rogers). Among their projects is the Centre Georges Pompidou in Paris. From 1977 on he collaborated with the engineer Peter Rice (Atelier Piano & Rice), and since 1980 he has been working together with Richard Fitzgerald.

Renzo Piano received the *RIBA* Gold Medal for Architecture in 1989 and the *Pritzker* architecture prize in 1998.

FLORIAN SAUTER VON MOOS

Born 1978 in Bregenz, Austria. He was an exchange student to Juneau, Alaska in 1994 and studied architecture at the ETH in Zurich. After graduation in 2004 he worked on several competitions, among others the University Library in Freiburg im Breisgau (with Heinrich Degelo, 2006, 1st Prize) and the Museum of Modern Art in Warsaw (with Christian Kerez, 2007, 1st Prize).

Since 2006 Florian Sauter has been a research assistant at the chair of architecture and design of Josep Lluis Mateo at the ETH in Zurich, where he is currently conducting his dissertation on "Louis I. Kahn and Nature".

FREDERIC SCHWARTZ

He was educated at the University of Berkeley (BA, 1973) and at the Harvard Graduate School of Design (M.Arch, 1978). Between 1976 and 1978 he worked for Skidmore, Owings and Merrill in Boston. Afterwards he joint the office of Robert Venturi and John Rauch in Philadelphia. From 1980 to 1985 he was the director of the New York office of Venturi, Rauch and Denise Scott Brown. In 1985 he was recipient of the *Rome* prize in architecture and founded his independent office in New York. His work has been shown in many international exhibitions, including the Venice Biennale (1986 and 2002). He has taught architectural design at Princeton, Columbia, Harvard, Yale and the University of Pennsylvania.

Frederic Schwartz was part of the *Think* team entry (in collaboration with Shigeru Ban, Ken Smith and Rafael Vinoly) in the competition for the redevelopment of the World Trade Center at Ground Zero (2nd Prize). He is currently planning the September 11, 2001 memorial "Empty Sky" in New Jersey.

RAMIAS STEINEMANN

Born 1976 in Zurich, Switzerland. He studied architecture at the ETH in Zurich and graduated 2004 as a diploma student of Jacques Herzog and Pierre de Meuron. In 2002 he was a collaborator in the research project "Switzerland – An Urban Portrait" at ETH Studio Basel. He has worked in the offices of Luigi Snozzi (Locarno), Vittorio Gregotti (Milan), OMA Asia (Hong Kong), Christian Kerez (Zurich) and Güller & Güller Architects (Zurich). In 2007 he opened together with Steffen Lemmerzahl and Lukas Kueng his independent architectural practice *SLIK*. Just recently they have won a honorable mention in the international competition for a Museum of Modern Art in Warsaw (2007).

Since 2005 Ramias Steinemann has been an assistant teacher at the chair of architecture and design of Josep Lluís Mateo at the ETH in Zurich.

PETER ST.JOHN

Born in 1959, he studied at the Bartlett and the Architectural Association school of architecture in London. He worked for Florian Beigel and Arup Associates prior to establishing his own office with Adam Caruso in 1990.

Both partners taught at the University of North London from 1990-2000 and were visiting professors at the Academy of Architecture in Mendrisio from 1999-2001. Since 2002 they have been visiting professors at the University of Bath. They also taught at the Graduate School of Design in Harvard (2005). Since fall 2007 they have been guest professors in architecture and design at ETH Zurich.

PHILIP URSPRUNG

Born 1963 in Baltimore, MD. He studied art history, general history and German in Geneva, Vienna and Berlin. He has been professor for modern and contemporary art at the University of Zurich since 2005. He has read at the ETH in Zurich, the Universities of Geneva and Basle, as well as the University of the Arts in Berlin. In 2007 he was visiting professor at the Graduate School of Architecture, Planning and Preservation at Columbia University, New York.

Philip Ursprung is the author of *The Limits of Art: Allan Kaprow and the Happening, Robert Smithson and Land Art* (Munich, 2003), publisher of *Herzog & de Meuron: Natural History* (Montreal and Baden, 2002) and co-author of *Images: A Picture Book of Architecture* (Munich, 2004).

MARIA VIÑÉ

Born 1972 in Kassel, Germany. She received her degree in architecture from the University in Kaiserslautern in 1998. In 1996 she was an exchange student at the Ecole d'Architecture Paris-Val-de-Marne and received the 1st Prize in the international student competition "Forum de la Jeune Architecture". After graduation she worked with Josep Lluis Mateo in Barcelona. In 2004 she founded with Martina Voser their independent architecture and landscape office *VIVO*. She received the European *Bauwelt*-Prize ("The First House") for a winery in Aranda de Duero, Spain, in 2006.

Maria Viñé has been an assistant teacher at the chair of architecture and design of Josep Lluís Mateo at the ETH in Zurich since 2003.

ERWIN VIRAY

Born 1961 on the Philippines. He was educated at the University of the Philippines (BA, "cum laude"), the Kyoto Institute of Technology (M.Arch) and the University of Tokyo (Doctor of Engineering in Architecture). Between 1991 and 2002 he lectured at the Kyoto Institute of Technology. Since 2002 he has been assistant professor in the school of design and environment at the National University of Singapore (NUS). In 2005 he was a design critic at the Harvard Graduate School of Design.

Erwin Viray has been an editorial associate with the architecture magazine *a+u* in Tokyo since 1996. He was editor and author of the issue "Herzog & de Meuron: 2002-06".

The next issue of
ARCHITECTURAL PAPERS MONOGRAPHIES

will be called

25 HOUSING ICONS SINCE 1980

and will be available in
JULY 2008